Boardwalk Memories

Boardwalk Memories

Tales of the Jersey Shore

Emil R. Salvini

INSIDERS' GUIDE®

GUILFORD, CONNECTICUT
AN IMPRINT OF THE GLOBE PEQUOT PRESS

INSIDERS' GUIDE ®

Design by Linda Loiewski

Map © The Globe Pequot Press

Library of Congress Cataloging-in-Publication Data

Salvini, Emil R.
    Boardwalk memories : tales of the Jersey shore / Emil R. Salvini. — 1st ed.
        p. cm.
    Includes bibliographical references and index.
    ISBN 0-7627-3674-7
    1. Atlantic Coast (N.J.)—Social life and customs. 2. Atlantic Coast (N.J.)—
Description and travel. 3. Atlantic Coast (N.J.)—Biography. I. Title.

F142.A79S25 2005
974.9'85—dc22   2005046018

Manufactured in the United States of America
First Edition/First Printing

Summer afternoon — summer afternoon . . .
the two most beautiful words in the English language.

—Henry James (1843–1916)

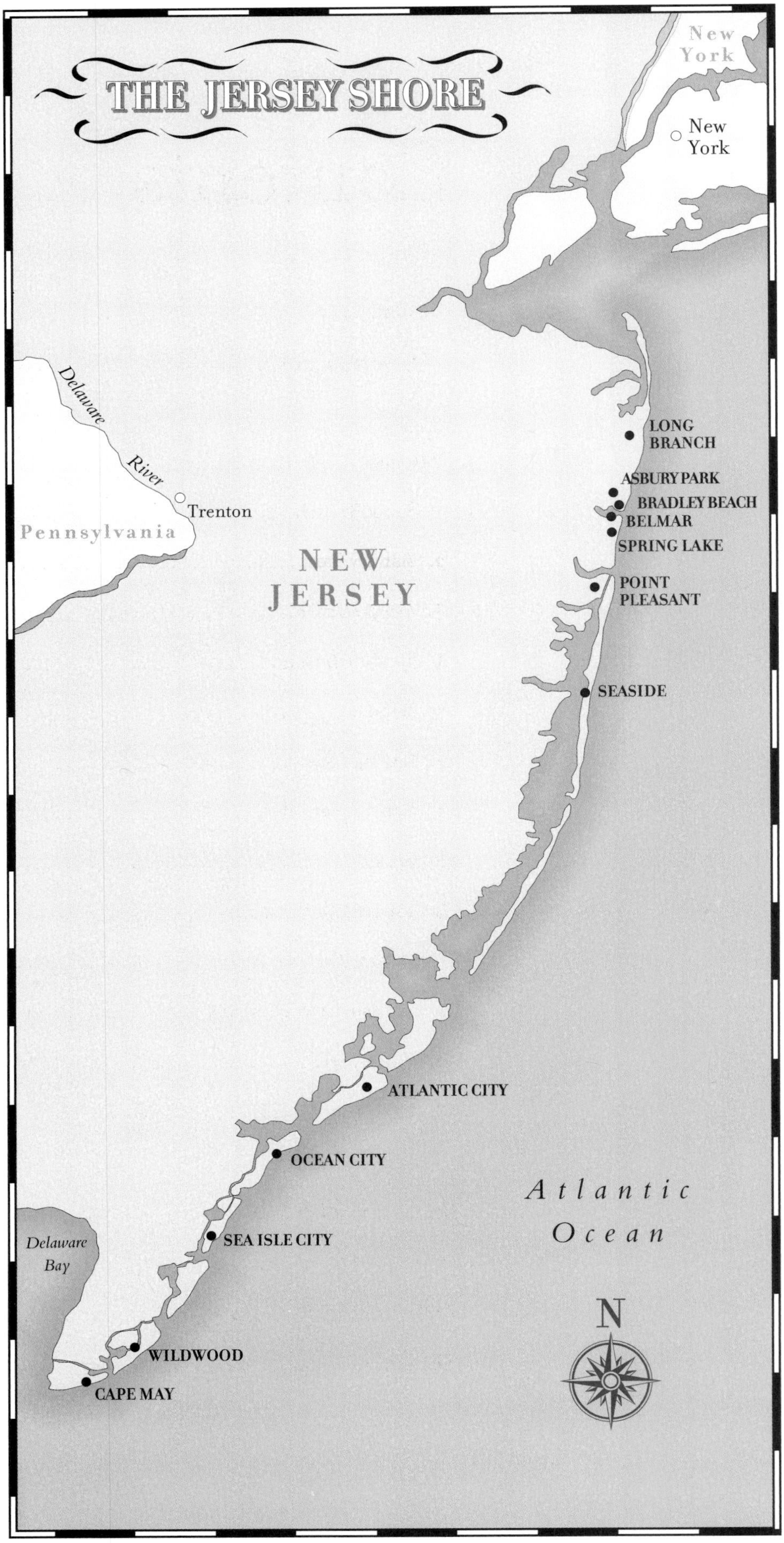

THE JERSEY SHORE

New York

New York

Delaware River

Trenton

Pennsylvania

NEW JERSEY

Delaware Bay

LONG BRANCH

ASBURY PARK

BRADLEY BEACH
BELMAR

SPRING LAKE

POINT PLEASANT

SEASIDE

ATLANTIC CITY

OCEAN CITY

Atlantic Ocean

SEA ISLE CITY

N

WILDWOOD

CAPE MAY

Contents

Preface

One of my fondest childhood memories revolves around a visit to the Jersey Shore. I had just turned seven, and my parents gave me permission to spend a week with my grandparents at their summer home in Bradley Beach. I had never been to "The Shore," as New Jersey residents refer to the 127-mile coastline from Sandy Hook to Cape May Point, but I eagerly anticipated a week of the beach, sun, fishing, biking, and especially spending time with my wonderful grandfather.

I was not disappointed. It was late June, and the days were hot, the evenings cooled by a light breeze. I awoke with the sun and immediately began to pester my grandfather to take me to the beach. I vividly remember walking along the wooden walkway from Bradley Beach through Ocean Grove to our destination: the bustling Asbury Park boardwalk. That summer marked the beginning of my lifelong love affair with the boardwalks of New Jersey.

I recall being both mesmerized and a bit frightened by the two cavernous structures that anchored each end of the great Asbury Park walkway. We strolled along the boards from the Casino to the Convention Hall, and my eyes grew wider by the minute as I took in all of the ways to invest the coins my grandfather had earlier stuffed in my pockets. The cacophony of music, laughter, bumper-car collisions, bells, whistles, and the mechanical sounds from the busy arcade were a "kid symphony" to my young ears. The games, the rides, the magical carousel, and of course the dizzying ambrosia of the cotton candy, suntan oil, hot dogs, and peanuts hooked me immediately. I played my first game of Skee-Ball that summer; years later I would introduce my daughters to the challenge of rolling wooden balls down the allies of the ancient machines. Each machine begrudgingly yielded the coveted prize tickets that my children would horde all season to cash in for their boardwalk treasures on Labor Day.

Today the Jersey boardwalks vary in size and length from a few hundred feet to miles. To generations of shore lovers they are emblematic of the Jersey Shore. Some preserve the honky-tonk, circus-barker, neon midway atmosphere, while others have become peaceful promenades along the sea. Most are as popular as ever, while some desperately search to reinvent themselves and recapture their glory days. Love them or hate them, they are an important and unique part of New Jersey culture, and every year a new crop of children, like that young boy in Asbury many summers past, discover their magic.

Acknowledgments

I extend my gratitude to all of those who made this book possible. I am especially indebted to my research assistant, Ann Stahl. Ann joined the project in midstream, filling in the gaping holes left by previous researchers and forging ahead with enthusiasm, determination, and skillfulness. Her work was essential to the completion of the book. Special thanks are due to my wife, Nancy, who walked every boardwalk on the Jersey Shore with me and cheerfully accompanied me on my frequent excursions to libraries, historical societies, and museums. I am grateful for her steadfast belief in me and for inspiring me at every turn.

To the following friends, family members, collectors, research staffs, and colleagues, thank you for sharing information and resources, for scrutinizing the manuscript and providing insightful comments, and for providing support and encouragement, especially toward the end of this endeavor: Peter Lucia, Curtis Bashaw, Robert Ruffolo Jr., Don Stine, Helen Pike, Tim Nagle, Mark and Susan Auerbach, Beth Wooley, Chris Lepore, Joseph Bennett, Christine Moore, Edward Worden, Frank Glaser, Linda Kay, Amy Salvini, Beth Salvini, Norris Clark, Robert Stewart, Ruth Smith, Hank Glaser, Paul Anselm, Laurie Gabriel, Mike Stafford, H. Gerald MacDonald, Robert J. Scully Sr., Bruce Minnix, Morey's Piers, Spring Lake Historical Society, William W. Wingard, Ocean County Historical Society, Dr. Floyd L. Moreland, Casino/Pier Breakwater Beach, Sea Isle City Historical Museum, Wildwood Historical Society Museum, Ocean City Historical Museum, Rick Zitarosa, Jenkinson's Boardwalk, Milton Edelman, Cape May County Historical Society, Barbara Hofstetter, Monmouth County Historical Association Library and Archives, Katherine Vonahnen, Shirley Ayres, Troy Bianchi, Ken Pringle, Anne Burrows, Larry Fishman, Kelly Reilly Ford, Mary Anne McAleavy, and Wheal-Grace Corporation.

I also thank the publisher, The Globe Pequot Press, and especially editors Mary Norris and Gillian Belnap; the manuscript benefited a great deal from their attentions.

Prologue

Visitors to Atlantic City in the 1860s wrote home of sand so deep in the streets that it reminded them of snowdrifts. The purpose of the first Atlantic City "board walk" was to keep sand on the beach and out of hotels, trains, and summer cottages.

It is impossible to think of the New Jersey seaside without calling to mind its alluring boardwalks. More than 31 miles of these uniquely American walkways of wood line the shore. They come in all sizes, ranging in length from just 200 feet to 5 miles. Some are still constructed of pine or cedar in the traditional herringbone pattern, whereas others are made of macadam or brick pavers.

Although they all share a common history, each boardwalk along the New Jersey coast has its own unique personality that reflects the resort that built it. The 0.7-mile boardwalk at Ocean Grove, for example, is noncommercial, mirroring the pious tone of the town, which began life as a Methodist meeting camp. Today it is frequented by those seeking a peaceful seaside saunter. Shore enthusiasts who are looking for a Jersey-style, heavy-decibel, neon-laden boardwalk experience need look no further than Seaside Heights, Ocean City, and Wildwood. These walkways abound with movie theaters, amusement piers, kiddy rides, souvenir vendors, and Skee-Ball arcades.

The boardwalks north of Long Beach Island today have a distinctly Manhattan flavor, with New York–style pizza, Italian sausage sandwiches, and Devils, Yankees, and Mets caps and jerseys in abundance. The boardwalks to the south serve as satellites of Philadelphia, replete with cheesesteaks, pork rolls, funnel cakes, and, naturally, Philly team memorabilia. Whatever your taste, there is a boardwalk that will suit.

The First Boardwalk

While the majesty of the Boardwalk at Atlantic City dwarfs all of the others (the city claims to have invented the concept of a boardwalk), historic records document a "flirtation walk" in Cape May in 1868, two years before the first wooden plank was laid on the sand dunes of its neighbor to the north. Although Cape May appears to be the first, no one can doubt that the boardwalk as we know it today evolved in Atlantic City. So important was the commercial value of that walkway that the city officially adopted the word *Boardwalk* with a capital *B* as a proper name in 1896.

The first boardwalk at Ocean Grove consisted of wood planks placed directly on the sand. Like many early boardwalks, the planks were removed and stored in the autumn.

Long Branch in the era before the town's first boardwalk was built. A series of wooden stairways led to the famous bluff. Hotels provided bathhouses and rented bathing garments to those who sought to escape the summer heat in the waves. Long Branch condoned coed sea bathing, while other resorts required men and women to swim separately.

Necessity is indeed the mother of invention, and the need to keep sand on the beach and out of hotels, railroad cars, and private residences gave birth to Atlantic City's first wooden walkway. Anyone with a beach house can

attest to the age-old battle of sand versus carpets, couches, beds, and even bathtubs. Sand seemed to be everywhere, and, as the population increased each summer, so did the problem. The city's permanent population in that era was less than five thousand people. The summer season added more than thirty thousand revelers to the population—all headed for the beach.

An enterprising pair of local businessmen sought to solve the problem. Jacob Keim, the proprietor of the Chester County House in Atlantic City, and Alexander Boardman, a conductor on the Camden and Atlantic Railroad and also a hotel owner, called a meeting of fellow businessmen and the press in the spring of 1870. They began the meeting by noting that strolling on the beach had become very popular among visitors to the resort. Early records indicate that swimming was dangerous without organized beach patrols, and most Victorians preferred a leisurely jaunt on the strand to an invigorating frolic in the surf. Keim and Boardman then went on to remind the group how the costly fine carpets and plush furniture that were a necessity in order to attract the best clientele to the fledgling resort were being destroyed by sand. First-class trains in the Victorian era were also finely appointed, and Boardman witnessed the same problems with sand in his elegant passenger cars.

"Flirtation walk" as it appeared in 1879 in Cape May.

Men, women, and children all enjoyed a stroll along Cape May's walkway of wood. Promenading on the boardwalk was a popular pastime in the late nineteenth century. An electric trolley paralleled the walkway all the way to Cape May Point.

The solution? Boardman and Keim proposed that the city provide a walkway of wood along the dunes to accommodate the strollers and keep their establishments as free of sand as possible. The idea was not new, although Boardman and Keim may have thought so: Two years previously, in 1868, the Cape May *Ocean Wave* had made mention that visitors of Cape May could "avail themselves of the privilege of a wide board walk of some thousand feet in extent." Boardman and Keim displayed illustrations of their new "board walk," along with a construction budget of $5,000. All present agreed that the walkway of wood was the answer to the problem, and on May 9, 1870, the city passed a resolution to build. Construction specifications called for 1½-inch-thick boards nailed to joists set crosswise, 2 feet apart. Each section was to be 12 feet in length and nailed to posts that projected just 18 inches above the sand. In autumn the 12-foot lengths were removed from the posts and stored on high ground until the following season.

The only opposition to the new plan came from several hotel owners who feared their view of the ocean could be impeded, should buildings be constructed on the boardwalk. The city calmed the hotelmen's concerns by adding a clause to the resolution that stated that no "bathhouse or shanty or building of any kind" was to be built within 30 feet of the walk and never on the ocean side without special permission from the city. Those early pioneers could never have imagined that by the twenty-first century colossal hotel-casinos would tower

over the wooden walkway, and that their owners—in an effort to create self-contained cities within the city and to keep guests at the slot machines and off the beach—would intentionally provide no view of the ocean just outside.

The first Atlantic City Boardwalk was dedicated on June 26, 1870, and as the crowd set foot on the new wooden walkway along Atlantic Avenue, a tradition was born: the Boardwalk parade. There were no rails on the first Boardwalk, and the papers reported that at least once a day someone fell off the new 18-inch walkway and "in nearly every instance the parties had been flirting." As the residents and tourists celebrated into the early hours of the following day, few of them could have realized that their "walkway of boards on the sand" would turn the white sand golden, and that boardwalks would one day become synonymous with the New Jersey seaside.

Nature's Fury

The Great Atlantic Hurricane of 1944 took the boardwalks of New Jersey to task for encroaching on Neptune's lair. Pictured here is the Asbury Park boardwalk after the hurricane.

When Neptune takes us to task for our hubris in building too close to his kingdom, the boardwalks of New Jersey have in many instances been the first line of defense. From Long Branch to Cape May, no walkway of wood has escaped nature's fury. The 127 miles of oceanfront have been defined and redefined by an endless procession of hurricanes and northeasters as we attempt to carve out a thin slice of paradise alongside the unforgiving Atlantic Ocean.

Boardwalks were not the only victims of vicious Jersey-coast storms. In 1896 a violent storm stranded the steamer *St. Paul* off the Long Branch beach. Indeed, the ocean floor off the New Jersey coast is so littered with the carcasses of shipwrecks and their treasure that the state is considered one of the best places in the world to conduct salvage dives. One estimate puts the number of ships lost off the Garden State coast at more than 875 from the period 1640 to 1935.

Since 1953 we have humanized these horrific ocean terrors by giving them sequentially alphabetical names, such as Frances and Ivan, and each year we pray that we will not make it to the end of the alphabet. Like a famed athlete's uniform number, we even retire the names of such superstars of destruction as Camille, Gloria, and Hugo. Each generation seems to remember a particularly destructive storm that becomes their "storm of the century"—at least until a new one claims the title. In the case of the New Jersey coast, two events stand out as heavyweight boardwalk killers.

The Great Atlantic Hurricane

The summer of 1944 was an optimistic time for the country. Americans closely followed the advance of the Allied troops that landed in Normandy, France, on June 6 and celebrated the declaration that the Battle of the Atlantic was officially over. Ships along the New Jersey coast no longer feared attacks from German U-boats, and the resort towns would soon be permitted to unveil the former brilliance of their boardwalk's amusement and concession stands. During the war U-boat blackout curtains had turned the traditionally dazzling walkways of wood into seaside specters. Now once again families crowded the hotels and boardwalks along the Jersey shore and cheered for Miss New Jersey at the Miss America contest in Atlantic City. The country was in a celebratory mood as the news spread that Paris had been liberated. People sensed it would be only a matter of time before their loved ones in uniform would return home, and they would once again experience the joys of summer on the "Jersey boards."

Unknown to the ocean lovers intent on squeezing a few more days from the unusually warm September was a threat looming in Neptune's lair more destructive than an armada of German wolf packs. Although on average one hundred tropical disturbances develop each year between May and November over the Atlantic Ocean, only twenty-five of these disturbances turn into tropical depressions. Of these depressions, only ten develop into hurricanes, and on average only two of these are likely to hit the Mid-Atlantic coast of the United States. Worse odds than a boardwalk wheel of chance, but in September 1944 the Great Atlantic Hurricane beat those odds and redefined the New Jersey coastline forever.

The fast moving, strapping hurricane was first detected on September 9 northeast of the Leeward Islands that stretch in an arc from the U.S. Virgin Islands to South America. Raising havoc for any ship that had the misfortune of crossing paths with the hell storm, it was quickly dubbed by meteorologists as the Great Atlantic Hurricane. By September 14 the center of the monstrous hurricane was headed near Cape Hatteras, North Carolina, and by the time it made landfall it was of category 3 intensity, packing winds from 111 to 130 miles per hour and traveling at a speed of 30 miles per hour. The New Jersey coastline had already been softened up by a few days of drenching rain that caused flood conditions from Cape May Point to Newark and Jersey City, and newspapers were predicting that there would be the devil to pay. By 5:00 P.M. on September 14, the Great Atlantic Hurricane was approximately 60 miles off the Delaware Bay. New Jersey was in for a night of uncharted terror.

Showtime began when the barometer dropped to 28.5 inches, and a towering storm surge hit the Cape May shoreline, wiping out the famous boardwalk in just under five minutes. Convention Hall and the seaward end of Hunt's and the Pennyland piers broke to pieces, transformed in seconds from fun palaces to low-flying missiles damaging everything in their path, including 200 homes, stores, and hotels. Beach Drive was transformed into what looked like a desert archeological sight, with remnants of concession stands, Skee-Ball games, and ornate boardwalk lampposts poking out from beneath 4 feet of sand. South Cape May, a small nineteenth-century town located between Cape May Point and Cape May, had been fighting erosion for years. This time the hurricane tore it to pieces and tossed it out to sea, and the charming seaside town vanished forever. Another treasured resource claimed by the storm were the scores of century-old trees that once lined Cape May's venerable streets.

The Asbury Park boardwalk looking north after the 1944 hurricane. Convention Hall, in the distance, sustained damage but survived the storm.

The next stop for the angry wind and water express was the town of Wildwood, where the famous boardwalk was fortuitously spared serious damage thanks to its distance from the Atlantic and the resort's unusually wide beach. Sea Isle City and Stone Harbor did not fare as well, their boardwalks turned to expensive kindling in just a matter of moments. The hurricane's next target, the historic Methodist Ocean City, became subject to a seemingly perverse joke as the formerly "dry" town was quickly submerged in more than 6 feet of water, its boardwalk afloat like some strange seaside logjam.

As the storm traveled north, it slammed into the narrow resort of Longport, where, despite the boardwalk being nestled inside a sturdy seawall, the wind and water sent boards smashing into the fragile homes along the sea. Next, the hurricane tackled the granddaddy of boardwalks, Atlantic City, crushing the walkway where just days earlier the Miss America Pageant had taken place. The city's oldest pier, Heinz Pier, was stripped to a wooden skeleton.

Long Beach Island was not known for boardwalks, but Beach Haven was proud of its 1¼-mile yellow pine walkway, constructed in 1917. It was actually the town's third boardwalk, the first appearing in 1896. The Beach Haven boardwalk was predominantly noncommercial, with only six enterprises and lines of nearby bathhouses, but by the time the Great Atlantic Hurricane had its way, every structure, including the fishing pier and boardwalk, were destroyed, with the exception of a handful of

Above: The Cape May boardwalk was demolished by the force of the Great Atlantic Hurricane of 1944.

Below: Residents of Ocean City stare in disbelief at their ravaged boardwalk and beachfront in the aftermath of the 1944 hurricane. Within a year barely any trace of the onslaught was visible. Homes were rebuilt on higher pilings, while others were stubbornly rebuilt on their original foundations. With the assistance of funding from the county, state, and federal governments, in a historic coastal rehabilitation program, Ocean City constructed bulkheads of wood and stone along the beach from 34th to 57th Streets.

bathhouses. Sadly, the community's beloved boardwalk was never rebuilt, as the salvaged decking was sold to wealthier Atlantic City for repairs to its damaged walkway.

Before the hurricane was satiated, it added the Ocean Grove, Asbury Park, Belmar, and Long Branch boardwalks to its list of victims. A 50-foot storm surge rolled the Asbury Park boardwalk, complete with its restaurants and amusements, into town, and city officials declared it a total disaster. Fortunately, although badly damaged, Asbury's casino and convention hall survived the onslaught.

Ocean Grove was ravaged, and all of the pavilions and the boardwalk were lost. Belmar had just celebrated the completion of a new pavilion and boardwalk—now all of it was history. Bay's Head's boardwalk vanished, and Point Pleasant's oceanfront became unrecognizable. The storm crushed Long Branch's venerable Chelsea Pavilion, and its boardwalk looked like a shredded and warped piece of saltwater taffy. Indeed, every single structure on Long Branch's beachfront was destroyed, including more than a hundred bathhouses. Keansburg and neighboring communities took the final brunt of the storm as it demolished more than fifty vacation homes. Understandably, the Great Atlantic Hurricane would be remembered as the most horrific and destructive twentieth-century storm to strike the coast of New Jersey—until the next one came along.

The Great Atlantic Storm of 1962

Memories of the Great Atlantic Hurricane grow dimmer as each year passes. Young children who witnessed that terrible storm rearrange the New Jersey coastline would be more than seventy years old today. Today when the subject of great storms is raised, people are more apt to remember the Great Atlantic Storm of 1962. This unique event did not stalk the coastline with the bravado of a full-fledged hurricane, but instead came quietly to destroy the New Jersey coast and wash centuries of history out to sea.

Monday, March 5, was a rather ordinary day on the New Jersey shoreline. The weather report for that day read "Monday: chance of rain, cloudy. Tuesday: cool and cloudy." The hurricane season had officially ended in November, and most conversations were about Lt. Col. John Glenn, who had made history on February 20 by being the first American to orbit the Earth three times aboard Mercury capsule *Friendship 7*.

The Heinz Pier in Atlantic City, built in 1886, as it looked in its prime.

The world-famous attraction was broken in two by the 1944 hurricane and never rebuilt.

A less friendly event was about to take place, and unlike a hurricane, there would be no warnings, no bulletins, and no evacuation notices. No one saw this storm coming. Although the term would not be coined until the end of the twentieth century, the March 1962 event, in meteorological terms, was a "perfect storm." All of the conspirators had to be aligned for this storm to cause the maximum amount of damage. The first participants were the sun, the moon, and Earth. There was a new moon, traditionally a time of high tides, and the sun and moon were in alignment. Perigee tides, higher than normal tides that occur every six or seven months when the moon is closest to the Earth, were the next culprits.

The horrific show began with force 10 and 11 winds battering the coastline, accompanied by a mixture of rain, snow, sleet, and hail. Before long 25- to 35-foot waves were slamming the shoreline. What made this storm so memorable and devastating was that it was no hit-and-run affair. Assisted by all of the conspirators, the storm systematically and slowly pounded the New Jersey coastline for three days and nights. Every successive flood tide—seven in all—washed another piece of history out to sea.

By the time the Great Atlantic Storm of 1962, as the U.S. Weather Bureau named it—or the Ash Wednesday Storm, as many locals dubbed it—finally headed north and the sun broke through the clouds, the New Jersey coastline was in shambles. Sand piled several feet high throughout all of the seaside towns, and familiar landmarks were either buried or washed out to sea. Vacation homes had been tossed around like weightless dollhouses. Cape May City's fifteen-block boardwalk was demolished, its Beach Drive transformed into a mass of blacktop debris, Convention Hall damaged beyond repair, and the famous Cape May strand gone altogether. In addition, each new tide flooded heating systems, causing pipes to freeze and burst in many homes.

The damage was similar all the way up the New Jersey coast. An initial damage estimate to private and public assets was more than $100 million—and that was in 1960 dollars. Twenty-one people lost their lives, and more than two thousand buildings were demolished. At Beach Haven, a Navy destroyer, the USS *Monssen*, was actually beached. The Loveland Town Bridge that spanned the Bay Head–Manasquan canal at Point Pleasant had collapsed. People who had experienced the Great Atlantic Hurricane eighteen years earlier agreed that the former hurricane had been usurped as the storm of the century.

THE GREAT ATLANTIC STORM OF 1962

Known as a northeaster, the storm was the evil stepchild of two weather systems—a powerful east-bound snowmaker born in the Midwest and a southern fire-eater forming off the coast of Georgia. The two systems joined forces and headed north to create havoc. Another plotter—an arctic cold front barreling down from Canada—entered the scheme just in time to insure that the beach-wrecker stalled long enough to gather its hurricane power.

A member of the Mollo family of Sea Isle City took these two photographs of the Women's Civic Club (in the distance on the boardwalk) during the Great Atlantic Storm of 1962. The left-hand photo shows the club building as the northeaster reached the coast. By the time the second photograph was taken twelve hours later, the club had fallen victim to the horrific storm.

Precise data on the Ash Wednesday Storm do not exist because, just as a thief covers his tracks at the scene of the crime, this storm had the audacity to destroy the weather recording equipment on the Steel Pier in Atlantic City, along with the tank that belonged to the famed high-diving horse. Longport lost almost 3,000 feet of its boardwalk and most of its fishing pier as the entire resort was submerged. Nearby Ventnor also lost its walkway. The storm gobbled up piers along the coast. Most of the famous Atlantic City hotels were flooded. Ocean City's beachfront was in ruins, and homes burned as submerged streets prevented firefighters from reaching the doomed summer dwellings.

The list of damage seemed endless: The Sea Isle City boardwalk was crushed, and almost 300 homes were lost to the successive tides. More than 1,000 feet of Long Branch's famous walkway was washed out to sea. Seaside Heights lost a major section of its boardwalk. In all, the storm had redrawn the New Jersey coastline forever. In Ocean County, the Atlantic cut through Long Beach Island to create three new channels to Barnegat Bay. In fact, Long Beach Island, from Barnegat Light to Beach Haven Inlet, was underwater for several days after the storm as 25-foot waves joined the Atlantic Ocean with Barnegat Bay. Eighty percent of Long Beach Island's structures were damaged or destroyed. The storm's tidal flooding and monstrous waves moved more sand than an army of bulldozers.

After the Great Atlantic Storm, several towns gave up on the idea of a fragile walkway of wood along the unpredictable Atlantic. Cape May and Sea Isle City rebuilt theirs as "promenades" or macadam seawalls, to form a barrier against the next inevitable storm of the century. Jersey towns had begun to learn that, in the battle with Neptune, their claim on the kingdom of sand dunes was tentative.

Long Branch

An early-nineteenth-century account described the beach at Long Branch as "a strip of fertile black sand several miles in length…the land adjacent to the ocean rises perpendicularly from the beach nearly twenty feet." This was the famous bluff, which many at the time compared to the cliffs around Brighton in England.

The third Long Branch pier was built in 1879 to accommodate steamships such as the luxurious *Plymouth Rock*, shown here discharging passengers. Round-trip fare from New York City to Long Branch was 60 cents. The Plymouth Rock was owned by the flamboyant Jim Fisk, who kept 250 canaries, each named after a wealthy friend, in gilt cages in the ship's opulent salon.

On the grounds of the Long Branch Historical Museum, a tiny, rather unremarkable structure passes the seasons almost forgotten by the residents of the city that once rivaled Newport, Rhode Island, and Saratoga Springs, New York, as the summer playground of the rich and famous. The single-room hut stands just 8 feet high and, while no one famous ever occupied the Garfield Tea House, as it is known today, it is emblematic of the sixty-year era when seven presidents of the United States summered in Long Branch.

It was the summer of 1881 when President James Garfield, less than four months after his inauguration, arrived at the Washington, D.C., railroad station to catch a train to Long Branch, New Jersey, to join his wife and family. The newly elected president had decided to follow in the footsteps of his presidential predecessors, Ulysses Grant and Rutherford Hayes, and had arranged for his family to spend the summer months in the Elberon Hotel. Tragically, as the president made his way through the crowded station, he was shot by a mentally unbalanced, disgruntled office seeker named Charles Guiteau.

Long Branch in 1871, when Ocean Avenue was the place to be seen, and the grand hotels were world famous. The bluff walk was not only a place for sea lovers to promenade, but it also provided access to the ocean and bathhouses.

The mortally wounded commander in chief remained in Washington for two months, while no less than six surgeons repeatedly botched numerous operations. It is often said that it was not Guiteau's bullet that killed Garfield, but rather his physicians. Because of the insufferable summer heat and an outbreak of malaria, Garfield's doctors and family decided to move the fragile president to Long Branch, where, far from the festering city on the Potomac, they believed he would have a better chance of survival.

Arrangements were made to transport Garfield to a comfortable cottage on the grounds of the Elberon Hotel, but his condition was so critical that doctors thought he might not survive the short horse-drawn ambulance ride from the local train station to the cottage. A bold plan was quickly hatched, and Long Branch residents and tourists alike made resort history by constructing a ⅝-mile spur railroad line connecting the terminal to the front door of the cottage where the stricken president was to convalesce. Less than twenty-four hours after the first spike was hammered, the president's car glided gently up to the front door of the cottage.

Garfield did not survive, however—he died just twelve days later. The second and final train ride on the miracle spur carried the deceased president's body to the Elberon station. Shortly afterwards the ties of the

Thousands of residents and tourists labored through the night of September 5, 1881, to construct a temporary track for the special train that transported the dying President Garfield from the Long Branch railroad station to his cottage in Elberon. Concerned crowds kept a constant vigil. President Garfield died on September 19, 1881.

famous spur were removed and sold to a summer cottager, who incorporated them into a structure known as Garfield's Hut, which he proudly displayed on his cottage grounds. The owner hosted tea parties in the hut, where, legend claims, he stored his cream and butter in an icebox accessible by a trapdoor in the cottage floor. Upon his death the building passed to his son, and eventually, after more than a hundred years of numerous moves and some neglect, Garfield's Hut, or the Garfield Tea House, was moved to its present location on the property of the Long Branch Historical Museum. The historic little structure is in good company, for the museum itself occupies what was once the St. James Chapel. The chapel/museum is also known as the Church of the Presidents, in honor of the seven U. S. presidents who had summered in Long Branch and worshipped there: Ulysses S. Grant, Chester A. Arthur, Rutherford B. Hayes, Benjamin Harrison, William McKinley, Woodrow Wilson, and James Garfield.

While the eyes of the country were on Long Branch during President Garfield's final days and the story of the miracle spur made national news, it was actually the wife of a president who first put the resort on the society map. Long Branch had been entertaining visitors for more than fifty years before the start of the Civil War. (There is still an ongoing dispute between Cape May and Long Branch regarding which watering hole was the first on the Jersey coast.) "The Branch," as it was referred to at the time, was far ahead of most of the other Jersey towns—most only windswept dunes—when Mary Todd Lincoln gave it the presidential imprimatur by spending ten days at the resort's finest hotel, the Mansion House, in August 1861.

The Rise and Fall of "The Branch"

To understand the rise and fall of this famous summer city, we need to keep in mind several key factors: the power of the presidency, gambling, America's ever-changing moral standards, and the fickleness of the public, especially the affluent. A boardwalk was late to arrive in Long Branch, partially because of the geography of the beachfront, and partially because the resort had been established for more than seventy years before the first "flirtation walk" appeared in Cape May. Before erosion and beach replenishment altered the seascape, the beach was described in the early nineteenth century "as a strip of fertile black sand several miles in length . . . the land adjacent to the ocean rises perpendicularly

President Grant and his family pose in front of the "summer White House" at Elberon.

A GENUINE AMERICAN IDOL

The first sitting president that the resort successfully persuaded to establish a summer white house at Long Branch was Ulysses S. Grant. Grant had visited the resort in the past, and although he enjoyed himself immensely, he was not one for the formal social atmosphere of the large hotels. In 1869 he told wealthy Philadelphia publisher and Elberon summer resident George W. Childs, "In all my travels I have never seen a place better suited for a summer residence than Long Branch." Soon thereafter, Childs, along with millionaire luxury railroad car manufacturer George Pullman and New York financier Moses Taylor, purchased a cottage at 991 Ocean Avenue and presented it to the president. At the time a Long Branch cottage was best described as a house that could be maintained with a small staff—so this was no mere bungalow.

Grant and his family loved the cottage, the water, and Long Branch life. For a dozen years, while in and out of office, Grant made seasonal visits to the resort. Realizing the value of a presidential association, the promoters of Long Branch managed over the years to persuade seven presidents to associate themselves in varying degrees with the resort.

Right: Work crews sinking the uprights for the new iron pier in May 1879. Fate was not kind to the new pier, however, and by 1881 it had washed away.

President Grant sea bathing in the Long Branch surf in the summer of 1869.

from the beach nearly twenty feet." This was the famous bluff seen in the early illustrations of the Long Branch beach and compared by many at the time to the cliffs around Brighton in England. A series of wooden stairways led the bather from the top of the bluff to the beach and bathhouses. Until the need to build a boardwalk was established in the early twentieth century, a series of piers served a similar purpose. As each pier was claimed by ocean or accident, a new, more robust one was constructed.

In the summer of 1870 the resort took a gamble on an event that would skyrocket Long Branch's popularity across the nation. Monmouth Park opened for business on July 4 and held its first horse race to the thrill of the thousands who witnessed the winners claiming opening day purses and stakes of the princely sum of $31,000. The hotelmen realized the track meant increasing profits and happily contributed to the handsome purses. The gambling houses of Long Branch prospered and multiplied as Monmouth Park attracted boatloads of bettors.

The track also provided a place for women to make small wagers in an era when a lady's reputation could be destroyed by setting foot in a gambling house. After a few scandals over some questionable racing calls, Monmouth Park was reorganized in 1878 and again hit the ground running. A favorite visitor to the track was President Grant, who, along with other politicians, enjoyed the excitement of the races. Financier and philanthropist "Diamond Jim" Brady was often accompanied by the actress Lillian Russell to his private box at the track. The newspapers could not get enough of his antics—like the day he bet on the last horse in the race because he thought a friend by the gate had given him the thumbs down sign. Only after winning $32,000 on the long shot did Brady learn that his friend was merely suggesting that Diamond Jim join him on the lower level.

Gambling was legal at the time in New Jersey, and Monmouth Park helped Long Branch's numerous gambling houses to proper. One estimate put the amount

Above: The steamboat *Columbia* docks along the Iron Pier on a long-ago summer afternoon.

Right: Long Branch's claim to fame was Monmouth Park, where the rich and famous enjoyed the sport of kings—horse racing. Here Diamond Jim Brady thrilled the public when he won $32,000 betting on a long shot. The closing of the track due to a prohibition on gambling in 1897 signaled the town's end as a national resort.

wagered in a single season in Phil Daly's famous Pennsylvania Club establishment at between $5 million and $10 million. Regular visitors to the club included former president Grant, President Arthur, Congressman William McKinley, and soon to be vice president Garret A. Hobart. Wealthy businessmen such as George Pullman, William Vanderbilt, Jay Gould, banker Jacob Rothschild, and railroad magnate Chauncey Depew also loved the excitement of the Pennsylvania Club.

With the Monmouth Park racetrack growing more popular each season and the gilded gambling houses filled to capacity each evening, it appeared that Long Branch had become the Monte Carlo of the Jersey coast. Newspapers routinely reported that the hotels were overflowing with guests. After jamming cots in dining halls, parlors, and restaurants, the joyous hotelmen would be forced to erect tents on their vast lawns. On July 5, 1880, the *New York Times* reported that on one smoldering July weekend, *Plymouth Rock*, the pride of speculator Jim Fisk's luxury passenger fleet, was forced to return to New York City, "laden down with persons

who had intended to stay over the 4th and 5th, but who were unable to find accommodations anywhere." At least they could return to the sweltering metropolis in style. The *Plymouth Rock* was akin to a 345-foot floating hotel, with thirty-two luxury suites and a brass band. Wealthy friends of Fisk were serenaded in the dining salon by 250 canaries housed in gilt cages, each named after one of Fisk's friends.

Long Branch seemed to have it all, but, although considered a serious contender to Newport and Saratoga Springs, events were taking place that would eventually topple the high-flying resort. Although almost imperceptible at first, a change was taking place in the bustling hotels. The old-line New York and Philadelphia families that had originally established Long Branch were growing weary of the "sports" and "fast trade" that the racetrack and gambling houses were attracting, and slowly they began to abandon the Branch. Before long, the grand old resort by the sea was bleeding bluebloods, all while the newspapers reported how business could not be better. As the gambling trade grew, middle-class

A view of the pier and crowded beach on a summer day circa 1930. The pier was the scene of trendy marathon dances during this era.

A busy spring afternoon on the boardwalk. Merchants had clearly discovered the commercial value of the wooden "street."

excursionists came in droves to watch the show, and when the horseless carriage first appeared on Ocean Boulevard, Diamond Jim Brady had a custom rig built to his specifications. Not one to disappoint his public, Diamond Jim asked for the headlights to be installed inside the car instead of out front. After all, he was the show.

As the "400" crowd—Long Branch's movers and shakers—began to summer elsewhere in increasing numbers, James Bradley, the founder of Asbury Park, and his associates in the Anti-Race Track League began a protracted battle against the gambling interests in Long Branch. It should be noted that there had been a fierce economic rivalry between the two popular resorts, and some historians believe that Bradley's motives were not based on moral convictions alone. After a few early losses against the powerful gaming promoters, Monmouth Park was closed down in 1893. Any hope for a gambling comeback—the tract reopened briefly—was dashed when, in 1897, a state constitutional amendment was adopted banning bookmaking and gambling. Horse-racing was still legal, but wagering was not, and as the bookmakers who had been paying $10,000 a day to the track vanished, so did the track. One by one the plush gambling establishments also closed their doors.

The golden age of Long Branch that began with presidential summer residences had come to an end. The fast money was not interested in the health benefits of the ocean or quiet evening strolls on the promenade. They headed instead for Long Branch's old nemesis, Saratoga Springs, where betting on horse racing was still legal. The majority of those who valued the peace and quiet of the seaside had abandoned the Branch years earlier to escape the dandies, actresses, and gamblers. The middle-class weekend excursionists who came to see the show left disappointed. The word was out—after more than a century as the premier resort in America, Long Branch was no longer "in."

In order to survive, this once-fashionable seaside escape soon realized it needed to copy the model of more modern resorts such as Asbury Park and Atlantic City. Schemes were attempted to replace horse racing. For a time automobile racing became a fad, then horse shows, dog shows, indoor balloon racing, cakewalk exhibitions—everything was tried in an effort to bring back the crowds.

The newspapers of the day expressed the need for a new amusement pier and a boardwalk, and the fifth and final pier was built in 1908. Although it promised to be a first-class amusement attraction along the lines of the great amusement piers of bustling Atlantic City, the funds needed to create the dream pier could not be raised. Instead, town leaders chose to remove the carcass of the old Iron Pier and build a modest amusement and fishing pier in its place.

Long Branch struggled to re-create itself while newer resorts were in their prime. By the late 1920s, promoters floated the phrase "the New Long Branch" in major metropolitan newspapers. The town indeed changed, becoming more diverse in the first two decades of the new century as Italian and Jewish families sought to enjoy the dream of a home by the sea. Many of the Italians originally came to Long Branch in the late nineteenth century to construct and maintain the famous gardens of the John Hoey Hotel and estate, which featured a world-class, tree-lined park and a unique 40-by-80-foot living flower carpet designed to be viewed from the hotel porches. So popular were his gardens that Hoey issued admission cards to control the crowds.

As the town settled into modest optimism, a bizarre event took place that sent the resort into a tailspin for decades. Rather than welcoming the new hardworking ethnic citizens and the promise they represented, many of the longtime residents chose the ugly path of the burning cross and white hood, and one of the largest Ku Klux Klan contingencies in New Jersey took root in Long Branch. Their hatred for Catholics, Jews, and other ethnic groups culminated on July 4, 1924, with a mass march through the town. Reports of the time state that so numerous were the cowardly, hooded marchers that the parade took four hours to pass through. Bright and early the next day Jews and Catholics boarded their homes and left Long Branch in droves. Shops closed and businesses folded as the town almost self-destructed in the venomous atmosphere. As the residents realized what the Klan had done to their town and businesses, they turned on the hateful organization, and it all but disappeared from the region.

In the mid-1930s Long Branch gambled again on a racing scheme, this time, dog racing. The state granted a license, and gambling returned to the Branch for the first time since 1893. The action took place at night under hundreds of electric lights in Ocean Park. Although some might have argued that dog-racing enthusiasts were not the kind of trade the humbled resort needed, they did temporarily energize the beach-

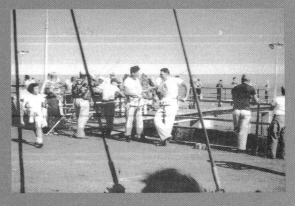

Above: The Long Branch fishing pier provided fun and relaxation for generations of families. Today it is a boardwalk memory.

Center: The boardwalk and pier with Max's famous hot dog stand on the right. Max's opened on the boardwalk in 1928. It burned in the great fire of 1987 but was rebuilt and is today is located at Ocean Boulevard and Matilda Terrace.

Below: The boardwalk and pier fire of 1987 destroyed dozens of amusements, restaurants, and shops, as well as the boardwalk and fishing pier.

front. But within a few years the State Supreme Court ruled pari-mutuel gambling illegal, and dog racing ended in Long Branch. The track promoters brought a new fad to the track, midget car racing, that survived to 1952. The track was eventually torn down to make way for a hotel in the early 1960s.

The Long Branch Boardwalk

Long Branch's boardwalk began late in the life of the resort. There was no apparent need to invest in an amusement-style boardwalk as long as gambling was the major draw. With the closing of the track and the decline of the gambling clubs, Long Branch sought other ways to keep the hotels and beaches full. In 1898 Pleasure Bay Park was created by a steamboat and railroad conglomerate seeking to increase off-peak travel on their ships and trains after the racetrack was closed. Located at the convergence of Branchport Creek and the South Shrewsbury River, it was a favorite day trip for those staying in the beachfront hotels and a convenient harbor for the wealthy to park their yachts. Pleasure Bay Park evolved into a popular picnic grove and amusement area, complete with a merry-go-round, dance pavilion, pond for summer and winter boating, and floating theater.

The town looked forward as it received a new charter in 1904 and became a city. In 1905 the new city constructed the ten-acre Ocean Park on the footprint of the old Ocean Hotel. The park was a favorite seaside location where residents and visitors could enjoy the fountains, flowerbeds, and concerts. Tourists had been enjoying the resort for almost a century before the first planks were installed along the famous bluffs in 1906. In August of that year the *New York Times* reported that the new boardwalk "hereafter known as 'Bluff Walk'" was under construction and when completed would be 1½ miles in length. The plan included the construction of a casino in 1907 to accommodate conventions, exhibitions, and social events. It replaced the older Agricultural Hall, a repurposed exhibition hall from the 1876 Centennial Exposition in Philadelphia. By the late 1920s the opening of the Holland Tunnel by New York City contributed to automobile travel, and the pier and boardwalk concessionaires prospered. A new 2-mile boardwalk was completed in 1923, and in 1930 a fishing-boat landing was constructed at the pier. The year the city's casino was lost to fire, 1928, also saw the birth of a Long Branch tradition—Max's beachfront hot dog stand.

The restaurant has enjoyed cult status ever since, with oversize hot dogs and a "secret flavor" recipe.

The Long Branch walkway of wood never reached the proportions of rival resorts such as Asbury Park and Atlantic City. In 1951 the *Times* wrote how the Branch boardwalk amusement park was "a comparatively silent one" and that Asbury Park's boards were "greater, grander and gaudier." The same article described a custard vendor who joked that if he had the same concession stand at Seaside, he could buy two Cadillac automobiles at the end of the season instead of just one. A favorite on the boardwalk was the pokerino shop, where for 5 cents a player could roll a small rubber ball onto holes in a checkerboard and illuminate a poker hand. The most popular prize at the time? Cigarettes, though packs could be exchanged for other prizes.

The problem of erosion was addressed with the construction of a $1.5 million seawall in the late 1950s (funded in part with a $700,000 New Jersey State conservation grant). The city held up the seawall as a symbol of its fight against lost tourism, erosion, and a growing urban blight problem. Public housing began to replace many of the nineteenth-century structures that had fallen into disrepair. Various redevelopment schemes were proposed by successive city administrations, but with the exception of a few condominiums and a Hilton hotel, most floundered due to a lack of funding, proper planning, and community support.

Long Branch attracted unwanted publicity in the 1950s and 1960s when organized crime took a liking to the ailing resort. The famed head of New York City's most powerful crime family would hold court in the Polka Dot Lounge. Other bars such as the Surf Lounge, Jazz City, and the Paddock became known for their unsavory patrons. Numerous investigations took place, as state law enforcement officials expressed concern that organized criminals had cast a hungry eye on the investment opportunities offered by the city's abundant vacant properties and beachfront lots. The state stepped in, and over the next decade the struggling resort rid itself of its reputation as a Mafia haven.

By the 1980s the boardwalk was a collection of small amusements and games of chance, merchants, restaurants, and food concession stands anchored around the old fishing pier. The major attraction, Kid's World Amusement Center, opened in 1985. Principal owner

Miniature golf became a craze during the Great Depression, and no self-respecting Jersey shore resort was without a course or two. That the Branch took to miniature golf in a big way can be seen by this massive facility that straddled the boardwalk in the 1950s.

Pat Cicaiese called it "an amusement park for the twenty-first century," where children could bounce on trampolines, climb rope webs, crawl through rooms packed with tennis balls, and—when their bodies were exhausted—spend some time in the computer area learning basic skills. Games of chance were to be replaced with interactive games for children. Admission for the park was set at $7.95, and plans were for the pier amusement park to encompass the existing Haunted Mansion and the Chelsea Pool and waterslide across from the boardwalk. The emphasis on a more upscale, less honky-tonk atmosphere was designed to attract family-oriented tourists to the depressed resort. The city scheduled a press conference and along with Cicaiese proudly pre-

dicted how the park would bring 500 new jobs to the amusement area. There appeared to be an uneasy truce between the politicians who viewed the commercial boardwalk as an outdated blight on their redevelopment plans and others who cherished the roller coaster, the fishing pier, and the ambrosia of hot dogs, pizza, peanuts, and suntan lotion as the soul of their city.

Sadly for the latter, a fire destroyed the commercial center of the boardwalk on June 8, 1987. Fanned by the gale force winds, the conflagration consumed Fisherman's Pier, the Haunted Mansion, the brand-new Kid's World, Shooter's bar, a small roller coaster, and a group of restaurants, bars, and souvenir shops. Spared were adjacent

A view of the Long Branch boardwalk as it appears today. Although the June 8, 1987, fire cleared the way for today's ambitious redevelopment, many believe that the heart and soul of the resort was lost on that day.

businesses Jimmy Liu's Café Bar, Wizard's World pinball arcade, and Gifted Sara, Long Branch's answer to Asbury Park's Madam Marie. Although these attractions survived, the 1987 fire was the end of the resort's commercial boardwalk. Politicians toured the ruins, including the governor, and pledged financial aid as the underinsured boardwalk operators pleaded for assistance. When the smoke cleared a year later, the pier, along with the 150-foot gutted section of the old boardwalk, remained in ruins. The mayor told the press that the fire would not affect the city's plan for redevelopment, and when asked by a reporter if the boardwalk would be restored, Gifted Sara smiled and said, "I see condominiums."

The fortune-teller knew her stuff. The old-fashioned walkway of wood is gone, along with the sounds of roller coasters and boardwalk barkers. Long Branch has been experiencing a major gentrification as the city ushers in one of the most ambitious redevelopment programs in the nation. The city gained national attention as it sought to attract developers by creating "the Long Branch rule," a bold plan that allows developers who meet local guidelines to comply automatically with state law. This was accomplished by incorporating all of the state's development regulations into Long Branch's local zoning laws. In another first, the New Jersey Department of Environmental Protection signed into law a blanket permit for the ambitious redevelopment

plan. Developers could now gain fast-track approval by the New Jersey Coastal Area Facilities Review Board, the group that vets all coastal development. Instead of the normal one-year waiting period, a developer could now expect a forty-day approval, once the local planning board gave the plan the green light. The message to developers was loud and clear—both the state and city were able and willing to move quickly on plans for a new Long Branch. They enacted what then-governor Christine Todd Whitman referred to as "a pledge to get out of the way."

Change can be difficult, and a redevelopment plan of this scale has proven disruptive to the older and lower income residents who find themselves in the way of the wrecking ball. The city is testing the boundary lines of eminent domain as it seizes homes and properties, not for schools or hospitals, but for upscale town houses and commercial space. Some property rights scholars question whether the redevelopment plan is based more on increasing tax revenues than on the redevelopment of an urban area for the public good. A few dozen holdouts cling dearly to their homes decorated with NOT FOR SALE and EMINENT DOMAIN ABUSE signs. Most know that they will eventually lose the battle and be forced to relocate, as they will be unable to afford the new condos and town houses that will line the seaside. Gifted Sara's vision of "I see condominiums" proved prophetic. Was she truly gifted, or did she, like many, just follow the smart money?

Asbury Park

Asbury Park occupies one of only two spots along the New Jersey shoreline—Long Branch to Manasquan—where the mainland meets the ocean. Cape May, a hundred miles to the south, occupies the other. The majority of New Jersey's seaside resorts are built on barrier islands, mere strips of sand.

Asbury Park was the first city in New Jersey to operate an electric trolley. Pictured here is the Sea Shore Electric Railway, circa 1900.

On a bright, sunny day in July 1894, Sterling Elliot, the editor of the periodical *Good Roads*, was attending a convention in Asbury Park when he found himself in the midst of a sea of spectators preparing to enjoy the annual baby parade. Unsure of the cause of the commotion, Elliot flagged down a local policeman. "What's up?" he asked the frantic constable, who, after giving an incredulous look, replied tersely, "Baby show." Like some kind of rube who had just arrived from the hinterlands, Elliot had stumbled upon a city event that at its peak drew more than 100,000 spectators to the mile-long Asbury Park boardwalk.

The first baby parade held in Asbury Park on July 22, 1890, had 200 children competing for the grand prize of—what else?—a baby carriage. What a sight it must have been: the bands serenading the oceanfront crowd with "Rock-a-Bye Baby," while Asbury's founder, James Bradley, carrying his trademark white umbrella, leading the red, white, and blue caravan. The fearless judges of that first parade awarded prizes to those they deemed the handsomest babies. By the time Sterling Elliot visited Asbury Park, the current crop of judges had decided it would be less dangerous to judge the best decorated carriages rather than the physical attributes of the occupants.

The Asbury Park Baby Parade was a major attraction from the first event in 1890 until the last infant march in 1949. The red, white, and blue tribute to children and motherhood drew more than 100,000 people in 1910. Presidents Theodore Roosevelt and Woodrow Wilson viewed the national event on separate occasions.

Bradley's "City by the Sea"

Only twenty-four years before this endearing picture of Americana rolled down Asbury Park's boardwalk, the land that they paraded on was a seaside wilderness overgrown with oaks, pines, and cedars, and inhabited by only one family. A pious, wealthy New York City brush manufacturer named James A. Bradley carved Asbury Park out of this rustic landscape. He was attracted to the natural beauty of the land, noting how Asbury Park occupies one of only two spots along the New Jersey shoreline—the region from Long Branch to Manasquan—where the mainland meets the ocean. The picturesque village of Cape May, a hundred miles to the south, occupies the other. The remainder of New Jersey's seaside resorts are built on barrier islands, mere strips of sand. To the casual observer of the day the handsome tree-lined avenues made one wonder if this were truly the Jersey shore or some country village.

Bradley's association with the Jersey Shore began in 1870 when he purchased a lot in Ocean Grove, a "tent village" founded only the year before by the Methodist Camp Meeting Association. As a devout Christian, Bradley feared the land bordering Ocean Grove would

TILLIE AND THE LEGACY OF CONEY ISLAND

The origin of the Asbury Park's "Tillie" face is a story in itself. In 1897 George Cornelius Tilyou created the famed Steeplechase Park in Coney Island, New York. Legend has it that the original clown faces adorning that building bore a strong resemblance to Tilyou and his brother Edward. The clown face became a Coney Island trademark that was used on tickets, in advertising, and as signage for the rides. The popularity of Tilyou's Steeplechase Park on Coney Island spread to several major resorts in New Jersey, including Asbury Park and Atlantic City.

The Asbury Park Steeplechase (above), located on Ocean Avenue between 2nd and 3rd Streets, began operation in 1880. (The building fell to the wrecker's ball in the 1930s.) This circa 1915 photo of the amusement shows two different but similar images of the Steeplechase trademark clown face grinning madly at the passing pedestrians. The Asbury Park Steeplechase was a place where turn-of-the-twentieth-century revel-

ers could throw off their Victorian constraints. A popular Steeplechase attraction was the Human Roulette Wheel, a spinning circular platform that would tumble a hundred seated strangers into a pile of mixed-gender humanity—extremely risqué behavior in an era when single women were expected to travel with a chaperone! The two demonic jesters depicted on the building promised a daring brand of amusement for unattached men and women seeking a summer flirtation.

The clown face morphed over the years, eventually evolving into the Palace Amusements' "Tillie" jester (left), an image embedded in the souls of thousands of children and adults who recall the magic of the Palace amusements at night and the demonic, grinning face of Tillie calling all "board rats" to the tunnel of love and his other delights.

By the time Leslie W. Thomas was hired to paint this New Jersey icon, the Asbury Steeplechase was long gone. In a 1998 interview, Thomas told a reporter that he had been provided with a clown design that he used as a starting point for Tillie. Little did he know that the image would someday be depicted on T-shirts, coffee cups, calendars, and several Hollywood and television productions.

fall into the hands of a secular promoter who might not share the values of the association. When almost 500 acres just north of Wesley Lake came on the market in 1871, the entrepreneur purchased the land for $90,000 and promptly named the area Asbury Park, in honor of Bishop Francis Asbury, the first bishop of the Methodist Episcopal Church ordained in the United States.

Bradley was an energetic and resourceful man who carefully planned the layout of his "city by the sea" before the first tree was felled. Even today, visitors to Asbury Park can sense that the 100-foot-wide avenues that flare to 200 feet at the ocean were not randomly measured, but followed the nineteenth-century footprints of someone

who sought to maximize the ocean views and sea breeze throughout his city. "Founder" Bradley, as he was known to the town's residents, also set aside land for parks, churches, and civic structures, and incorporated city planning concepts that he encountered while traveling through Europe. Bradley was so determined to make his enterprise a success that he sent coaches to meet the train in Long Branch and transport sojourners to Asbury Park in the years before the railroad extended south to his fledgling resort.

His planning reached beyond aesthetics, making Asbury Park in 1881 the first seaside resort in America to have a sanitary sewer system. Six years later came the community's

Left: Local author Helen-Chantal Pike recalls a rite of passage at Asbury Park: riding the Casino carousel at age ten. "Could I fit in another big-girl ride? I counted my tickets and headed for the Casino. No tiny horse-and-pony merry-go-round for me. I wanted the real thing. The classic Philadelphia Toboggan Carousel. It was housed inside a specially built semi-circular room of glass and verdigris, its outside walls surfaced with howling Medusa-like medallions. Inside, the majestically carved horses were nearly life-size; my feet barely made the stirrups. The organ started playing, the platform began to revolve." Pictured is the evocative entrance and the long-lost magical carousel.

Above: A generation of Asbury Park tourists and residents remember the Morro Castle. The luxury liner ran aground on the beach at the resort on September 8, 1934. More than a third of the 455 people on board lost their lives in the tragedy. The massive ship beached adjacent to Convention Hall and the boardwalk, presenting a surreal spectacle. The cause of the fire that doomed the popular cruise liner has remained a mystery for more than seventy years. The Morro Castle eventually burned to a gutted shell.

trolley network, the second electric system in the United States and the first in New Jersey. Prior to this all trolleys were horse drawn. By 1889 Bradley's city was becoming known the as the Duchess of the North Shore, second only to its neighbor to the south, Atlantic City. Asbury Park's permanent population of more than 4,000 residents swelled to 30,000 during the summer months, people who could now stroll its expansive avenues and shoreline in the evening under the welcoming glow of electric street lamps. One estimate for the 1883 season calculates summer visitors at more than a half million.

A dozen hotels were constructed to accommodate vacationers, and hundreds of private and guest cottages dotted the tree-lined streets. The city also supported three newspapers and three banks, plus an opera house, library, and lecture hall. By 1890, as a testament to the popularity of Asbury Park, several of the hotels remained open throughout the winter months.

In 1877 a 1-mile, primitive boardwalk was constructed and connected to Ocean Grove, creating an uninterrupted promenade of 2 miles. As in most seaside towns, the first boardwalk, or "plank walk," was portable and stored at the end of each season. Contemporary reports tell of a quite narrow wooden sidewalk rather than a boardwalk. The first substantial elevated walk, constructed in 1880, varied in width from 16 to 32 feet. Bradley provided his tourists with benches spread along this boardwalk every 10 feet. He also constructed the city's first covered pavilion, near Asbury Avenue. Called the Bradley Pavilion, or simply the Asbury Avenue Pavilion, it provided a venue for band concerts and the first boardwalk retail enterprise, a candy shop. Stephen Crane, author of *The Red Badge of Courage*, who spent part of his childhood in Asbury Park before gaining literary fame, wrote in 1896 that "the very heart of the town's life is at the Asbury Avenue pavilion."

Bradley also constructed a fishing pier just north of the pavilion and—with his flair for the unusual—added a saltwater tank complete with sea lions to thrill the excursionists. Soon thereafter, in 1888, Ernest Schnitzler built a 100-foot-square enclosed pavilion at the inter-

The Palace Amusements' carousel dazzled generations of children with its hand-carved menagerie of horses, goats, camels, giraffes, and deer along with a pair of chariots and cherubs. The carousel figures were auctioned off when the Palace closed in the 1980s.

Above: Peter Lucia, author of the mystery novel *The Murder at Asbury Park*, spent his childhood in Asbury Park. He lovingly recalls it as a "storybook place" where the "boardwalk stripes the ocean's sandy edge and is weighted in place by the most fantastic pavilions." Peter grew up with his now-famous uncle, Danny DeVito, and they are both pictured here sharing a merry-go-round ride next to the boardwalk.

Right: The Stone Pony, one of the most famous rock clubs in America, is a "must stop" on a Bruce Springsteen pilgrimage.

section of Cookman Avenue and Kingsley Street to house his carousel and amusement hall. This was the origin of Palace Amusements, originally known as the "Kingsley Street Merry-Go-Round," an institution that would become emblematic of Asbury Park for generations of adults and children. (One such individual was Bruce Springsteen, who immortalized the Palace in such songs as "Born to Run," "Tunnel of Love," and "4th of July, Asbury Park [Sandy].")

The major attraction was the beautiful carousel crafted by Charles Looff, one of the first great American carousel artist. Seventy hand-carved animals—including horses, goats, camels, giraffes, and deer—spun in unison with cherubs and chariots as they transported seventy-eight travelers to a magical world of bright lights and deafening organ music, all for the price of admission. A lucky few who snagged the brass ring took another trip, compliments of the Palace.

In 1895 Schnitzler responded to demand for additional attractions with the Roundabout and Observatory. He designed and installed a Ferris wheel in a new structure situated just west of the carousel house. What made the new attraction so unique was how the upper portion of the giant wheel rose high above the roof in a north–south orientation, providing passengers with glorious views of Asbury Park and the Atlantic. He even added an observation platform, where voyagers could step off onto the deck when their carriage was at the wheel's zenith. What a sight the wheel must have been at night, covered with more than 500 lights on the observation tower and wheel!

The Crystal Maze—a hall of mirrors—was added in 1903, and in 1932 a second carousel was installed in the Casino building, across the street along the boardwalk. In 1956 came the Fun House and Bumper Car Building, along with its signature wall paintings, a series of bumper cars, and the two large fun faces. One face, outlined in neon,

became affectionately known as Tillie, a wild eyed, semi-demonic clown face that became synonymous with the Palace Amusements and Asbury Park.

When the Palace began its 1903 Crystal Maze expansion, the city of Asbury Park had been under the control of James Bradley for thirty-three years. That year—when the city council convinced Bradley to sell the beachfront to the city for $100,000—marked a turning point in the resort's history

The city council then hired famed landscape architect Frederick Law Olmsted Jr. to help the city shed its stodgy, nineteenth-century image. Olmsted's aggressive plan resulted in the razing of piers, bathhouses, and the orchestra pavilion. They were replaced with the Casino building on the southern end of the boardwalk and the Fifth Avenue Arcade at the north. A new boardwalk constructed that year extended a mile from Wesley Lake to Deal Lake. Seventy feet wide for more than ¼ mile and 42 feet wide at the narrowest point, the new pride of Asbury Park was of narrow white pine and, as the *New York Times* reported, "protected by an ornamental galvanized iron railing." The city celebrated the new walkway's opening in grand style as sundown approached, with dozens of

An evening of music and the expectation of a sea breeze attracted many resort visitors. Pictured is a Victorian-era concert on the Asbury Park boardwalk, where men and women sit together but notably apart.

Asbury Park, complete with rolling chairs, presented a serious challenge to Atlantic City in the early twentieth century.

The boardwalk was a magnet for celebrities promoting their latest project. In 1952 Dagmar, television's original glamour girl, rode the mile-long Asbury Park walkway in a roller chair.

arc lights lighting the boardwalk as hundreds of citizens promenaded to the strains of "In the Good Old Summertime," courtesy of the Old Monmouth Band.

Glory Days

Asbury Park continued to prosper throughout the first half of the twentieth century. The second and present Casino complex appeared at the southern end of the boardwalk in 1929, after the first was lost to fire. Plans to erect a hall to attract the lucrative convention business, discussed since 1916 through years of political contention, finally came to fruition when Convention Hall, located at the northern end of the boardwalk, opened for business on June 1, 1930. The massive structure by architects Warren and Wetmore, the designers of the Biltmore Hotel and New York's Grand Central Station, crosses the boardwalk and projects into the Atlantic. In its heyday the hall hosted the bands of Glenn Miller, Gene Krupa, and Tommy Dorsey, among others, and was the site of a fad of the era, dance marathons.

During the second half of the twentieth century it showcased such big-name acts as the Rolling Stones, the Doors, and Mr. Asbury Park—Bruce Springsteen.

But by the mid-1950s the Duchess of the North Shore had begun to show signs of age. Changes in modes of transportation from train travel to automobiles had a profound effect, as tourists no longer stayed for weeks at a time but instead came just for a day or two via the newly opened Garden State Parkway and New Jersey Turnpike. The age of the day-tripper had arrived. Many of the venerable hotels were forced to close their doors, and a downward spiral began, each business failure setting the stage for another. In July 1970, Asbury Park's decline was hastened by a race riot that resulted in hundreds of arrests and injuries and over $1 million in property damage. The message spread: The Duchess had been dethroned.

After a half century of despair, a feeling of optimism now caresses the resort like a gentle sea breeze. A true renaissance is in the works. The city government

Ice-skating over the beach. A rare 1950s photograph of the rink that once occupied the boardwalk casino.

has finally extricated itself from the failed developer, and in August 2001 a new company, Asbury Partners, was named master developer for Oceanfront Asbury. The ambitious fifty-six-acre, $1.25 billion public/private project is expected to be completed in phases over a ten-year period and promises to restore Asbury Park to its former glory while creating thousands of full- and part-time jobs for the depressed community. Asbury's Stone Pony nightclub, synonymous with Bruce Springsteen and numerous other New Jersey celebrities,

was purchased by Asbury Partners in July 2003 with plans for restoration as part of Oceanfront Asbury's entertainment rebirth. In 2004 the old boardwalk was demolished and replaced with pressure-treated southern yellow pine boards in the traditional herringbone pattern. While residents and fans of the former Duchess of the North Shore are taking a wait-and-see position, there is a sense of optimism that Asbury's Glory Days may soon return.

Ocean Grove

Ocean Grove began life in 1870 as a Methodist camp-meeting resort. In summer more than six hundred tents were pitched throughout "the grove," earning it the title "little canvas village." Canvas dwellings are still erected every summer and leased to the faithful. Many have been maintained by the same families for generations.

The bluest of the Ocean Grove laws—forbidding Sunday driving—was enforced until 1979, when the New Jersey Supreme Court ruled it unconstitutional for the Camp Meeting Association to govern the resort.

The nineteenth century gave birth to numerous experimental communities that sought an answer to the materialism of the industrial revolution. Ocean Grove began life as one of these, built as a Methodist camp meeting/tent village resort in the style, both architecturally and morally, of Oak Bluffs on Martha's Vineyard, Massachusetts. So plentiful were the tents in the early years that Ocean Grove was fondly referred to as the "little canvas village." Camp meetings and revivals had become part of the American culture since the first meeting was held in Kentucky in 1799. The Ocean Grove meetings would follow previous models with ten days of prayer, testimony, hymn singing, and sermons held at the end of August.

Nineteenth-century camp-meeting tents. In summer more than 600 tents were pitched throughout Ocean Grove, earning it the title "little canvas village." Canvas dwellings are still erected every summer by the Ocean Grove Camp Meeting Association and leased to the faithful. Today just 114 remain, many occupied by tent families who have been summering in "the grove" for generations. The occupants are expected to support the activities of the association, from attending religious services to manning the counter at a book sale. Often photographed for their history and charm, these canvas summer shelters are in great demand.

Eden by the Sea

Legend states that the elders of the Methodist Camp Meeting Association traveled the 127 miles of the New Jersey coastline searching for their slice of Eden by the sea. Their quest eventually took them to a peaceful location where the woodland met the sea. The elders were so moved by the beautiful grove of hickory, pine, and cedar trees they found there that they named their new paradise Ocean Grove. The diminutive resort was effectively cut off from the world's evils by two lakes and the Atlantic Ocean, and this suited the elders just fine. The founder of Ocean Grove, the Reverend William B. Osborn, purchased eleven seaside acres for $50 in 1869, and the first meeting was held that year by Dr. Ellwood Stokes on July 31 at what is now called Founder's Park. A charter was issued to the Ocean Grove Camp Meeting Association on March 3, 1870, and the association was granted all of the rights and responsibilities of a city government.

The new resort was a resounding success, and by 1872 the association owned more than 230 of the 300 cottages that had been built. In excess of 40,000 people visited the meeting grounds in 1874. One year later, the New Jersey Southern Railroad extended its tracks from Long Branch to Ocean Grove, and the public responded —more than 300,000 arrived the following summer. Ocean Grove founder Osborn is credited with overseeing the construction of the first auditorium and Ocean Pathway, the 1,500-foot-long majestic parklike vista that gently widens from 200 to 300 feet as it connects the auditorium to the sea. A new "setback" concept to ensure maximum sea views for the faithful was also employed in laying out the cottage lots for the first two blocks that paralleled the ocean. Every new structure

A favorite location on lazy summer days was the community fishing pier located off Embury Avenue. The pier at the southern end of the boardwalk, affectionately referred to as "The Magnificent Pier" by members of the Ocean Grove Fishing Club, was destroyed by a vicious northeaster in 1992. Just a year earlier, in 1991, the town had celebrated the one hundredth anniversary of the pier.

was successively "set back" from the adjoining property so that the resort appears nestled along the Atlantic. Dr. Stokes was elected president of the association in 1869 and held the office until his death in 1897. Stokes had more to do with the success and creation of Ocean Grove than any other person.

The new resort also caught the attention of politicians, celebrities, and authors—as much for its prohibitions as for its camp meetings. When listing his personal finances for the public in 1887, James Garfield noted that "in 1872 we took quarters at Ocean Grove. We rented a cottage and spent the summer there." Frederick Douglass spoke at the National Education Assembly held at Ocean Grove in 1883. In 1876 Olive Logan wrote for

Harper's New Monthly Magazine that there were "no balls, no bars, no late hours, no dissipations of any sort." She added that "visitors to Long Branch do not feel they have seen the 'lions' until they have driven down to Ocean Grove." She also described how the community, "a sort of poor man's paradise," closed the gates on Sundays and how visitors to Sunday camp meetings after the gate closing "quit their carriages on the shore of the little lake [Wesley], and are smuggled over—not very surreptitiously—in row boats for a one cent fare." She added that the meetings would often be held on the beach, where "the surf makes music in harmony with the human chorus." Wesley Lake became a thoroughfare for visitors with two ferryboats, one at New Jersey Avenue and the other at Pilgrim Pathway.

A nineteenth-century illustration of the Ocean Grove boardwalk. The octagonal building on the right is the camera obscura, where visitors entered a darkened room to watch images of the world outside projected on the surface of a small round table. A hand-operated rotating lens at the top of the tower provided viewers with 360 degrees of changing views of the hotels, ships, boardwalk, and streets of Ocean Grove.

An 1880s view from the Asbury Park shore of Wesley Lake looking toward Ocean Grove. Rowboats and canvas-top crafts were the only way to commute between the sister resorts before the iron pedestrian bridges were constructed. The large hotels seen in this photo attest to Ocean Grove's popularity only twenty years after the resort was created.

Ocean Grove continued to grow into a community of charming hotels and Lilliputian-style cottages. The Ocean Grove Camp Meeting Association never sold but rather leased the approximately 30-by-60-foot building lots for ninety-nine years at $10.50 a year. The size of the lots limited the scale of the structures, so for the most part the resort avoided the massive Victorian-style "cottages" popular at other contemporary seaside towns. The center of Ocean Grove was, and continues to be, the Great Auditorium, which was expanded during the late nineteenth century to accommodate the growing population. The present structure was completed in 1894 in just ninety-two working days by contractors who agreed to not work on the Sabbath and to abstain from profane or foul language on the work site. The Great Auditorium is beautiful and when filled to capacity has accommodated up to 10,000 worshippers for special events. The facility has hosted U.S. presidents Theodore Roosevelt, William McKinley, William Howard Taft, Ulysses Grant, and Richard Nixon. Other notables have included Billy Sunday, Billy Graham, William Jennings Bryan, Enrico Caruso, W. E. B. DuBois, and John Philip Sousa. A humorous blue law anecdote involves President Grant, who arrived in Ocean Grove in 1875 by carriage to address veterans of the Civil War and their families. The president of the United States—and former scourge of the Confederacy—discovered that, as it was Sunday, the gates to the resort were chained. No exceptions. With style and grace he dismounted from his horse, tethered his ride to the gate, and respectfully walked the rest of the way to the event.

The Boardwalk

During the early days of the resort, a group of small tents were erected on the North End beach to accommodate bathers and provide makeshift bathhouses. By 1877 two local entrepreneurs, Joseph Ross and Theodore W. Lillagore, leased bathing concessions from the Ocean Grove Camp Meeting Association and constructed the resort's first pavilions. The Ross Pavilion was located at the northern end of the beach, and the Lillagore Pavilion

A rare photograph of the Ocean Grove boardwalk at the Ross Pavilion in 1904. Canvas-awning boats are docked along the boardwalk waiting to ferry passengers across Wesley Lake, and camp-meeting tents can be seen in the background. "Bathing Pictures" were available at Pach Brothers photography studio; this firm was responsible for many of the only known examples of local seaside life in the Victorian era.

was erected on the southern end. The original pavilions were traditional double-decker structures open to the sea air, appointed with numerous benches to provide a peaceful haven for those seeking a cool retreat.

The pavilions were also connected with the town's first boardwalk, a 2,835-foot-long, 6-foot-wide wooden plank walkway studded with twenty-one lamps. For the first few years the boardwalk was taken up and stored at the end of the season. Then in 1880 a wider boardwalk replaced the original walkway and spanned the 3,257 feet between Fletcher and Wesley Lakes. The cost for the new promenade was just over $3,000.

A major attraction along the boardwalk for years was the camera obscura. Author Stephen Crane described the attraction in 1892 as a "scientific curiosity," where "people enter a small wooden building and stand in a darkened room, gazing at the surface of a small round table, on which appear reflections made through a lens in the top of the tower of all that is happening in the vicinity at the time." Those who entered the tiny structure were treated to miniature views of the streets, boardwalk, hotel porches, sea bathers, or a passing ship. The scenes were changed intermittently by the camera operator, who directed the lens mounted at the top of the building.

A 1940s view of the North End Hotel complex. The Scenario theater is now the Strand, where Shirley Temple's latest movie is showing. The pony track is gone, and the boardwalk has been extended around the hotel.

Ironically, it was the association's inflexibility regarding the Sunday driving law that eventually broke their rigid control of the resort's government. For decades they had successfully fought off all challenges. A proposal to construct an ocean boulevard connecting Ocean Grove with Asbury Park to the north and Bradley Beach to the south was rejected because the association feared it would encourage motorists to challenge the Sunday driving ban.

The demise of the Sunday ban began with a challenge involving the freedom of the press clause of the U.S. Constitution and the delivery of newspapers after midnight on Sunday. An inconclusive decision by the New Jersey State Supreme Court that permitted newspaper trucks to run until 2:00 A.M. Sunday left both sides of the controversy dissatisfied. The association realized this

was the beginning of the end when a dissenting justice asked, "When did the First Amendment expire at 2:00 A.M. Sunday?" Proponents of the Sunday driving ban would later wish they had opened the gates for the newspaper trucks. But there was no way of putting the toothpaste back in the tube, and by 1979 the New Jersey Supreme Court took the controversy a step further and tackled the issue of separation of church and state that courts and legislatures had avoided for decades. The court decided that the Ocean Grove government was unconstitutional and terminated the civil powers wielded by the church-affiliated Ocean Grove Camp Meeting Association. The association's last effort to maintain control of Ocean Grove by seceding from Neptune Township failed in a township-wide referendum in 1981.

Tunnels under the boardwalks permitted sea bathers to walk from locker rooms to the beach in their bathing suits without crossing the boardwalk. Unfortunately, every storm packed the tunnels with sand, which had to be removed shovelful by shovelful.

Today Ocean Grove retains its Victorian character with the assistance of the Board of Architectural Review that was established in 1976. The board ensures that the community adheres to exterior design standards and that no development takes place that will destroy the uniqueness of the seaside village. As other vintage resorts tore down their cottages and hotels to make way for fast-food restaurants and oceanfront condominiums, Ocean Grove saw that their most precious resource was the charming, gingerbread-laden wooden cottages and commercial structures that transport residents and summer visitors to a peaceful nineteenth-century Eden by the sea. Like the historic landmark city of Cape May to the south, the residents of Ocean Grove realized that thoughtless development is just that. In the 1990s the resort enjoyed a major renaissance as young families fell in love with Ocean Grove and purchased and restored many of the homes, restaurants, hotels, and guesthouses. The Methodist Camp Meeting Association still owns all the property, and the 10,000-pipe Hope-Jones organ in the auditorium reminds all residents on Sunday that this is still God's Square Mile. The population is now richly diverse as people of all faiths, ethnic backgrounds, and sexual orientation have discovered the tiny Methodist village as the perfect escape from the cacophony and bright lights of the twenty-first century.

Bradley Beach

Bradley Beach has the dubious distinction of being the first resort in the country to charge admission to fenced-off public beaches. In the 1930s tags were sold to more than 30,000 people annually. The income was used to improve local transportation and other revenue-producing public conveniences.

The Bradley Beach boardwalk and oceanfront in the late 1930s, during its heyday. The resort had won the bet in 1929 that eager sunbathers would not mind paying for the privilege to enjoy the beach.

A chance meeting in 1870 between a successful broom maker and a member of the Ocean Grove Camp Meeting Association was to have a profound impact on the northern New Jersey coastline. James A. Bradley had prospered in the Smith and Bradley Brush Co., but the stress of building and operating the business had taken a heavy toll on his health. At one time Smith and Bradley was one of the largest brush manufacturers in the United States. Bradley was considering an extended trip abroad when he met David Brown and was enticed by Brown to consider the purchase of a lot in Ocean Grove, the Methodist camp-meeting resort. This was an era when the medical profession ascribed profound health-promoting benefits to the seaside climate. "If the statements of well-known physicians are to be believed, there is no duty that a father owes to his children greater than making arrangements to have them spend the summer months away from the crowded city," proclaimed a Jersey Shore pamphlet published in 1913. The writer speculated that the doctor's bills of those who remained in sweltering, overcrowded cities during the summer far outweighed the cost expended on a summer cottage by the sea.

The essential key to prosperity for a Jersey Shore resort was the railway connection and the trainloads of summer idlers that it guaranteed. In summer 1912, when this station was completed, there were eighty-five daily trains between New York and Bradley Beach, thirty-five on Sunday. It was now possible for weekend cottagers and day-trippers to make the journey from New York City to Bradley Beach in less than two hours.

Bradley promptly took Brown's advice and traveled to Ocean Grove. He fell in love with the location and immediately purchased a lot. A year later, in 1871, Bradley founded Asbury Park, a resort that at one time was second in size and popularity on the Jersey Shore only to Atlantic City. Although born and raised a Roman Catholic, Bradley would later be converted to the Methodist religion by his devoted wife, Helen Packard. He was known as an antigambling, prohibitionist crusader and originally established Asbury Park on the northern border of Ocean Grove to protect the religious haven from any encroachment by secular resorts such as Long Branch. Although not common knowledge today, Asbury Park was originally held to most of the same "blue law" standards as Ocean Grove, including no liquor, no gambling, and no sea bathing or trains on the Sabbath.

In 1894 Bradley was elected to the New Jersey legislature as a senator from Monmouth County. As senator, he eventually exacted his revenge on Asbury Park's rival to the north, Long Branch, by casting the vote that ended racetrack gambling in New Jersey. The 1897 law closed Monmouth Park for good. Having been Long Branch's major attraction, the loss sent the resort into a downward spiral.

Bradley Beach's first boardwalk was actually a brick walkway with the addition of benches and bathhouses, a necessity in an era when it was unacceptable to be seen anywhere but on the beach in your bathing attire. The top floor of the pavilion provided sea and beach views and a convenient spot to escape the midday sun. The brick walkway lasted until 1921, a year after Bradley Beach purchased the beachfront from "Founder" James Bradley. A traditional wood boardwalk was constructed in its place.

James Bradley's choice of brick proved prophetic. Today after battling a century of storms, the Bradley Beach boardwalk is once again made almost entirely of brick pavers.

Bradley's Ironfisted Rule

Bradley so loved his quiet section of the northern shoreline that he began gobbling up acres of land, including a fifty-four-acre tract south of Ocean Grove. The "Founder," as he became known, was not adverse to turning a profit, and his investments in New Jersey quickly added to his manufacturing wealth. In 1871 his pet project was to develop the tract with partner William B. Bradner. They dubbed the fledging resort Ocean Park but were soon advised by local postal officials that the name was too similar to other nearby resorts. Local legend claims that when Bradner was too modest to suggest his own name, a postal worker said, "You have a man down here by the name of Bradley. Why don't you call it Bradley Beach?"

Bradley cast a long shadow, and it soon became apparent that he would happily bestow his benevolent dictatorship on his namesake resort, just as he would with Asbury Park. To say the Founder was an eccentric would be an understatement. The resorts could govern themselves any way they chose, as long as it was his way. After all, he owned the entire beachfront, as well as most of the property in both towns. He could be a generous benefactor and would often donate, or sell below market value, land for churches, libraries, and other pet projects. Bradley realized that he needed to populate his resorts, so he often lent money to individuals to purchase lots for their summer cottages.

He did not permit dissension in the ranks. As an example, in 1888 the Law and Order League of Asbury Park declared that all businesses be closed on the Sabbath, with the exception of drugstores, which were to remain open to dispense essential drugs for four hours only. The pharmacists rebelled and took a firm stand: Either they be permitted to stay open all day on Sunday, or they would not open at all. In typical Bradley style, the Founder secured a store, filled it with patent medicines

The elegant LaReine Hotel was a Bradley Beach landmark for most of the twentieth century. The hotel could accommodate more than 400 guests in what was at the time the epitome of luxury. Every floor was equipped with public baths, and several rooms on each floor had private baths. An early-twentieth-century brochure advertised "running water, long distance telephones, electric lights, gas, large closets and elevtors." James Bradley was particularly fond of the LaReine, where he discovered an ally in the hotel's operator, Thomas F. Somers, a fellow Methodist and temperance leader. The LaReine Hotel, like many wooden giants that once lined the oceanfront avenues along the Jersey coast, was lost in a fire in 1974.

and drugs, and hired a pharmacist. To add insult to injury, he undersold the other druggists in town. The pharmacists held out for a few weeks before caving in. Bradley then closed his store.

If Bradley did not care for something, he merely banned it. In one case he passed an ordinance forbidding the sale of "Frankfurter sausages," or hot dogs, on the boardwalk. He also kept the local printing presses busy producing large-format signs bearing his latest missive. Pedestrians along the boardwalk were treated to his thoughts, such as "Modesty of apparel is just as becoming to a lady in bathing costume as in silk and satins." Another was aimed at the "love-struck maidens and youths" headed for a favorite local lovers' lane at the foot of Deal Lake, at the end of the boardwalk: "No one will be permitted to pass this sign after dark. The object of this rule is obvious to all." The *New York Times* declared, "Founder Bradley Opposed to Cupid" (no matter that Bradley was born on St. Valentine's Day in 1830).

Bradley's beliefs and idiosyncrasies were not always as innocuous as his opposition to summer lovers. In 1893 he waged a war against an Italian band that had been giving popular daily concerts on the boardwalk at Asbury Park, a favorite with crowds from Bradley Beach, Ocean Grove, and Asbury Park. Bradley shocked the residents and city council by announcing that, because he owned the beach pavilion, he would not permit the Italians to play there. He refused to give a reason. On another occasion he enraged the African-American community, as the *Times* reported, "by posting notice in his music pavilion at the end of his boardwalk, which skirts his beach, at the New Jersey Summer resort, that colored people are not wanted there." Bradley claimed that his order was aimed at the hotel waiters and staff who were monopolizing the best seats in the pavilion, but his racism was exposed when a prominent African-American attorney in Manhattan challenged him as to why the signs did not simply say "No servants allowed." The Founder ignored the question and instructed his boardwalk police to follow his edict.

While Asbury Park was under Bradley's thumb for many decades, Bradley Beach was able to expedite its autonomy. Bradley Beach learned from its older sibling's predicament and was able to benefit from the lesson. In 1903, while Bradley was posturing with Asbury's mayor over control of the beach and boardwalk, Bradley Beach took its first step toward independence by breaking off from Neptune Township and forming the municipality of Bradley Beach. In 1908 a 0.7-square-mile tract, including the area south of Sylvan Lake, extended the resort's boundaries when the residents of Neptune City passed a referendum to become part of Bradley Beach.

Like any resort along the coastline, a railroad connection was essential to succeed. Bradley Beach was fortunate to have the Jersey Central (New York and Long Branch) Railroad as a conduit for the lucrative tourist and cottage trade. The town was close enough to New York City to make it a reasonable commute for a family, usually with a father spending weekends at the cottage and returning to the office during the week. Railroad connections from the south saw to it that a fair number of Philadelphians frequented Bradley Beach. Like Asbury Park and Ocean Grove, the new resort incorporated blue laws during the early days that prohibited conducting business or sea

Bowling was a popular activity for Bradley Beach tourists and year-round residents. In a 1908 *New York Times* article, "Much Bowling at Bradley Beach," the reporter noted, "it is a sport that seems always to have appealed to them rather than the other summer pastimes." Pictured here is the exterior of the LaReine Hotel's bowling alley in 1917.

The LaReine complex also featured a carousel, requisite entertainment for every self-respecting resort town by the turn of the century. A casino completed the hotels offerings—as Bradley Beach's "great amusement center," it featured billiard and pocket-billiard tables and a slot-machine arcade, a favorite with the tourists.

bathing on Sunday. Fortunately for Bradley Beach, the Founder did not direct his full attentions to the seaside town. Still, he did own a good deal of the resort, and this made it difficult for the municipal officials.

It is interesting that, although Bradley had sold his interest in the Asbury beachfront to the city in 1903 for $100,000, he still owned the Bradley Beach shoreline more than a decade later. The borough would ultimately purchase the beach from Bradley a year before his passing in 1921 for $499,000.

The Growth of Bradley Beach

By 1912 Bradley Beach was a bustling seaside community. The beachfront LaReine Casino housed a bowling alley, billiard tables, carousel, and slot-machine arcade. During the winter of that same year, more than twenty new cottages were erected in anticipation of the summer season. A new train depot was built at a cost of $10,000, and contrary to Bradley's wishes, the trains were per-

mitted to stop in Bradley Beach on Sundays. Two rail lines, the New York Central and the Pennsylvania Railroad, assured a share of the New York and Philadelphia cottage business. At the height of the season, eighty-five weekday trains operated between New York City and Bradley Beach, thirty-five on Sunday. Add to that the fourteen weekday and four Sunday trains from Philadelphia, plus the steamer boats the railroads also operated, and it is obvious why the borough wanted to obtain their beach from Bradley.

Bradley Beach has the dubious distinction of being the first resort in the country to charge admission to fenced-off public beaches. To the dismay of beach lovers everywhere, a writer for the Works Progress Administration reported in the 1930s, "The plan of selling metal tags for admission to the beach has spread widely." The tags were sold to the more than 30,000 people who, before the new scheme was incorporated, visited the beach on weekends and used the oceanfront at no cost. The resort began plans to build a $250,000 bathhouse complex to force day-trippers to pay 25 cents to change

The Beach View Hotel and Pavilion was an early example of the enormous barnlike hostelries that literally sat right on the beach. These were not luxurious facilities like the LaReine Hotel, but they provided all the necessities such as bathhouses, hot and cold seawater baths, and even bathing suits for rent.

The Beach View Hotel did offer a huge saltwater pool. Throughout much of the twentieth century, oceanfront saltwater pools were part of the Bradley Beach experience and a matter of pride for the resort. The pools provided the health benefits believed to be associated with saltwater sea bathing without the danger of the unpredictable surf.

By 1935 the boardwalk was bustling with activity and bore little resemblance to the old brick walkway that it had replaced. The popular pavilions were named for the streets that met the oceanfront. Pictured here is the Newark Avenue Pavilion close to the Ocean Grove border.

A unique Bradley Beach boardwalk memory—tennis courts along the walkway circa 1950. This public facility was located at 2nd and 3rd Avenues. Cooled by the refreshing sea breezes, tennis players provided spectators with demonstrations of their athletic prowess. Judging by the height of the fence, a good many tennis balls ended up on the beach.

into their bathing suits in a city-owned facility, and not in an automobile. The cottagers and year-round vacationers were originally exempt from the new tag ordinance. The borough paved Main Street with brick and laid a double-track for the trolley. The busy cars ran every five minutes during the peak season and connected Bradley Beach with Asbury Park, Ocean Grove, Avon, Belmar, Spring Lake, and Sea Girt.

Fortunately, the resort was able to extricate itself from Bradley and do away with the arcane blue laws even before the Founder's death in 1921. This was a good move for local businesses, because Bradley once said in a violent argument concerning a proposal to permit the New York and Long Branch Railroad to stop in town on Sunday, "Once the trains stop in town, the next thing you know they'll be bathing here on Sunday." The same year that he died, the borough replaced the aging Bradley-built brick walkway that had extended from Fletcher Lake to Avon with a proper wooden boardwalk. It then invested money in the repair of Ellor's Pavilion, also built by Bradley twenty years earlier. These two events signaled a period of growth for Bradley Beach.

There was also a palpable difference between the resort and its pious neighbor to the north, Ocean Grove. Bradley Beach was a much more tolerant community, and it attracted a diversity of people. Visitors could hold hands on the boardwalk, drink beer, and swim on Sunday. While Ocean Grove and Asbury Park women were still forced to wear the infamous "Bradley bag," a heavy flannel bathing suit that covered the wearer from her neck to the end of her ankles, women at Bradley Beach dared to show a bit more skin. This is not to say that there were no limits. The New York Times carried a headline in 1926, "Bathing Girl Who Sheds Dress in Public Startles Beach: May Cause Stricter Law." Apparently a young woman arrived by automobile, walked out onto the boardwalk, and pulled her dress over her head, revealing a two-piece bathing suit. The summer crowd gasped as she "tripped down the boardwalk stairs, and ten seconds later was in the water." Within the hour an emergency meeting of the borough commissioners was organized, and an ordinance was proposed that would require visitors who were neither staying in a hotel nor renting a cottage to use the municipal bathhouse.

By 1933 thirteen years had passed since the resort had purchased the beach and boardwalk from "Founder" James Bradley. A new walkway had been built, this time in wood, complete with new pavilions. The illustration on the left is the pavilion at McCabe and LaReine Avenues at the northern end of the walkway—women walking the boards in their bathing suits would have appalled the "Founder," who had passed away in 1921 at the age of ninety-one. On the right is the stately Newark Avenue Pavilion—a place to relax, escape the sun, catch up on gossip, and enjoy the popular summer evening dances.

One of the commissioners said, "We are through with spectacles like this kind at Bradley Beach." Naturally, the hotel and cottage owners were pleased with this "Bradleyesque" position. The following year the town officials agreed that no censor would be required for the beach. It was reported that, because there was no "radical change in bathing costumes and the present attire of bathing girls is sensible and above criticism," the official beach censor could take the season off.

Hotels such as the LaReine and the Beach View were constructed, and business was brisk. The LaReine boasted four hundred rooms, elaborate public baths on each floor, running water, electric lights, gas, telephones, and elevators. In addition, there were hot and cold water sea baths, bathhouses for changing, a beach pavilion, and even bathing suits for rent. Visitors who sought more thrills than the bowling alley and carousel could provide visited nearby Asbury Park, where they could ride the toboggan chute or giant Ferris wheel. Because of Bradley Beach's proximity to its bigger neighbor to the north, the boardwalk never developed into a full-scale commercial center.

Fire was always a concern of the small wooden towns by the sea, and one struck in 1932, destroying the Bradley Beach Casino on the boardwalk between Newark and Park Place. In 1953 the town began to sponsor the ubiquitous baby parade, and a year later installed forty mercury-vapor lights along its boardwalk. It was quite a beautiful sight. There were handsome pavilions that housed concessions and small arcade games. Miniature golf was, and still is, available along the walkway, and at one time there was a small kiddie ride complex on Park Place just north of the golf area. In addition, two large open-air swimming pool complexes once stood along the boardwalk, attracting thousands during the busy summer months.

Located at LaReine and Ocean Avenues, the old landmark LaReine Hotel survived into the 1970s. Most adults today recall the penny arcade on Newark Avenue, a second arcade on LaReine Avenue, and the dance pavilion on Newark and LaReine Avenues. The arcades were favorites for tourists and residents alike to try their skill at pinball or Skee-Ball. The beachfront sector would soon change dramatically when in 1974 the seventy-four-year-old LaReine burned to the ground.

The 2nd Avenue Pavilion. Along today's popular walkway are a miniature golf course, a bandstand, and a few concession stands, where soft drinks and snack food are available.

Standing Up to the Klan

The Ku Klux Klan had been well established in rural New Jersey during the late nineteenth and early twentieth century, and many of the Klan's members took steps to ensure that certain seasonal residents and day-trippers were not welcome. Marches were commonplace, causing many new cottagers and tourists genuine concern, and many resort promoters loss of sleep over their investment.

Not to be deterred, two years later the Klan battled with Bradley Beach officials over their right to parade in the ethnically mixed city. Mayor Frank C. Borden Jr. tried to keep the hooded hatred out of the resort and arranged for fifty state troopers to arrive in town fifteen minutes after the first Klansman stepped foot in Bradley Beach. The Klan, headquartered at that time at an abandoned Marconi wireless station on the banks of the Shark River, or what the *Times* referred to as "Klan Haven,"

remained defiant. Apparently, and sadly, they had obtained permission from several other resorts to parade. When they applied for a permit from Bradley Beach, however, the courageous mayor informed them that they would first be searched for firearms, and then have their hoods removed so they could be easily identified. The state troopers would see that the mayor's orders were followed to the letter.

Fortunately, as the years passed, the full-time residents of the shore and outlying regions became more and more tolerant of their summer guests, and less tolerant of the hooded thugs among them. The Klan eventually withered and died in New Jersey through a lack of interest and growing intolerance for such hatred. The robust development of the rural sector, along with the assimilation of the summer visitors into the year-round communities, also hastened the Klan's demise. Bradley Beach evolved into the family-friendly resort of today.

The bandstand on Bradley Beach's current walkway.

The Good Fight

In the end it would be King Neptune that changed the Bradley Beach boardwalk most of all. Man-made barriers along the Jersey Shore, designed to protect one inlet or a beach, have in many cases harmed another. Bradley Beach is an example. The jetties that were built in the early twentieth century to protect the inlet of the Shark River have interrupted the ocean's natural flow, resulting in a buildup of beaches on the south side of the barrier. But resorts on the north side, like Bradley Beach, were starved of sand. The loss of beach made the town easy prey for nasty storms, and throughout the twentieth century the Bradley Beach walkway was the victim of numerous hurricanes and northeasters. Each time the town rebuilt. In 1938, when an unnamed hurricane struck the Jersey Shore, the *Times* wrote of Bradley Beach, "a section of the boardwalk which will cost $50,000 to replace was turned into driftwood by the storm. Unestimated [sic] damage was done to beachfront pavilions." The city, realizing the tourism value of the boardwalk, tenaciously rebuilt the damaged section. The Great Atlantic Hurricane of 1944 and the Great Atlantic Storm of 1962 once again damaged the boardwalk, the latter burying Ocean Avenue in 3 feet of sand and ripping the boardwalk to pieces.

The borough would seek assistance from the state and federal government when possible, but the maintenance of the boardwalk was a constant drain on the resort's coffers. In 1978, just four years after the LaReine Hotel fire, a vicious storm did $2 million worth of damage to the beachfront. Twenty-five-foot waves pounded the fragile boardwalk and beachfront for hours, and finally the southern end of the walkway crumbled into oblivion. The mayor told the *New York Times*, "It was just lost to the sea; it broke up and disappeared into the ocean." If that were not bad enough, the waves swept over a four-year-old bulkhead and destroyed a 300-foot wall of bathhouses. The storm was so severe that more than 700 feet of beach was lost, exposing a claylike hardpan. The town officials turned again to the state and federal government for assistance.

The city continued the good fight, but it was a losing battle. In 1984 a northeaster did over $1 million worth of damage to the Bradley Beach beachfront. The historic winter storm of 1992 reshaped the New Jersey coastline with 90-mile-per-hour winds and battering surf and destroyed Bradley Beach's beachfront, boardwalk, and bulkhead. The cost to the resort was estimated to be between $15 million and $20 million, and town officials finally cried uncle. In a 1997 *New York Times* report, the mayor noted that, although the town had been spending $40,000 to $50,000 annually to maintain the boardwalk, it was "rickety, fall-down and like a child whose hair had not been combed." The logic was simple. "We know the ocean is rising and coming inland, so we decided to retreat as well as get away from the traditional wood solutions," the mayor told the reporter. "Now 90 percent of our boardwalk is masonry, which is cool to

the feet, low maintenance, and has 20 times the life of wood." Joggers might not agree, as the unforgiving masonry jolts their knees, but there is little doubt that the Bradley Beach "boardwalk" will stand up to the next big storm. Gone are the penny arcades, Skee-Ball machines, and saltwater pools. The boardwalk is essentially noncommercial, with benches, gazebos, a handful of snack bars, a bocce ball court, and a miniature golf course. The big gazebo, or bandstand, is the venue for popular free summer concerts. Sadly, the old hotels along the beachfront have vanished over time, as have the dance pavilions and bathhouses. Along with neighboring Asbury Park and Long Branch, Bradley Beach fell into an extended period of decline in the 1970s. Luckily, a loyal group of homeowners and summer visitors kept the town's spark alive until the mid-1990s, when a quiet renaissance began to take place. With little fanfare,

A miniature golf course is one of the amusements on the new boardwalk.

This circa 1920 photograph shows Bradley Beach at about the time when the resort purchased the waterfront property from James Bradley. Today's modern masonry "boardwalk," with its low-keyed, noncommercial atmosphere, is interestingly reminiscent of the Bradley era.

families began to return, spurred on by affordable housing prices and a ninety-minute train ride to New York City. Busy Manhattanites realized they could jump on the 5:00 P.M. train after work and spend their evening on the beach or enjoying a cool drink on their peaceful cottage porch. The streets hummed with the sound of renovation, and new restaurants appeared along Main Street. Two local favorites, the Brunswick Bradley Beach Bowl center and the Beach Cinema, were discovered by the new cottagers (the locals always knew they were lots of fun). Local, state, and federal funding replenished the beach sand, and today Bradley Beach is a comfortable old slipper of a resort. It may lack the exclusiveness of Spring Lake or Deal, but to the wonderfully diverse mix of full-time residents and weekenders, that is just fine.

Belmar

In the early 1900s Belmar's oceanfront benefited from the construction of a jetty to stabilize the Shark River inlet. The jetty disturbed the natural northward flow of sand and caused sand starvation at Avon-by-the-Sea and Bradley Beach. Meanwhile, on the south side, Belmar's beautiful, expansive beach grew to enviable proportions.

The original Belmar boardwalk in the horse-and-carriage era. The Columbia Hotel can be seen on the right; Gordon's Pavilion is visible at the far end of the walkway.

Hey fellas, why not head to the Jersey Shore for spring break this year . . . we could go to Malta—or Wallmere, Shade, or even Elbro . . . they're all great places to party." Although the Jersey Shore is still a popular destination for spring break, today's sun-loving college students wouldn't find these towns on the map. That decision was made almost a century ago.

When town elders were renaming the tiny seaside community of Ocean Beach in 1889, all of these names were considered and, fortunately, rejected. A consensus was eventually reached and the new name announced to the anxious citizens: Ocean Beach would from that point on be known as the City of Elco. No one is quite sure where Elco came from, but the name only lasted for about a month. It seems an irate citizen pointed out to the town government that Elco meant "Hell's Cove." The mayor's wife stepped in with a solution and, in May 1889, Belmar, an Americanization of the French *belle mer* for "beautiful sea," was the name given to the town, and this time it stuck.

The Belmar beachfront and the Columbia Hotel under construction. The name Belmar, adapted from the French *belle mer*, meaning "beautiful sea," was chosen as the seaside village's new name in 1889.

While Elco remains a mystery, Malta was a name that held some meaning for Ocean Beach. On November 24, 1885, in one of the worst northeasters that ever savaged the Jersey Shore, the *Malta*, an iron-hulled, full-rigged cargo sailing ship, came aground on the Belmar beach. Crews of men from the Shark River and Spring Lake Life Saving Stations bravely battled freezing water and heavy seas to rescue the crew. While the ocean was pounding the *Malta* to pieces, the lifeboats and breeches buoy brought as many men to safety as possible. Still, despite these valiant efforts, several crew members were washed out to sea. The wreck of the *Malta* rests not far off Belmar's coast, opposite 9th Avenue. It makes sense that the town came close to naming the community Malta in honor of the gallant ship.

Early Days

What is today the borough of Belmar began life as a religious community. In 1872 a group of camp-meeting Methodists from Ocean Grove, whose beloved Eden by the sea was becoming too crowded for their taste, traveled south along the coast in search of available land. They found the southern shore of the Shark River inlet to their liking: The fishing was good, the gentle sea breeze refreshing, and the region quite remote. Like many towns along the shore to the north, the land had been previously owned by a few rugged farmers who had settled the area during and after the American Revolution.

The 10th Avenue Pavilion in 1890 after a northeaster.

Another view of the damage caused by the 1890 northeaster.

On August 31, 1872, forty-one of these seaside pioneers acquired land enough for what would be 161 lots and formed the Ocean Beach Association. The group took advantage of the blank seaside canvas that was presented to them and laid out twelve spacious avenues that each began on the shore of the Atlantic and terminated at the Shark River. They then built a simple bridge over the Shark River to connect their village to what would become another religious community, Key East, founded in 1883 as a Baptist version of Ocean Grove. This neighboring resort was reestablished as Avon-by-the-Sea in 1900.

Once founded, Ocean Beach began to expand as lots were subdivided, cottages erected, and almost twenty hotels built in an eighteen-year period. Like Spring Lake to the south and other shore communities, Ocean Beach benefited from the 1876 Centennial Exposition in Philadelphia. This was the era when labor was less expensive than building materials (wood, glass, and iron), so it made more economic sense to move the grandiose buildings than to destroy them. Six exhibition halls were dismantled, shipped by rail to Ocean Beach, and reassembled, usually with modifications. Some were large enough to use as hotels, while others served as stately cottages.

Belmar, which became renown in the late twentieth century as a rental resort, started this practice early in its history. Many cottage owners realized that they could rent their homes to city dwellers for sizable sums during the summer season by building small bungalows or cottage additions where they and their families could live rent-free.

Like most Jersey Shore resorts, a wooden walkway was built and a series of pavilions and bathhouses were constructed on the beach. Records indicate that in 1893 the Ladies and Gents Ice Cream Parlor was built by the Shark River Amusement Company. The amusement facility also provided fishing boats to rent, a shooting gallery, a Chute-the-Chute (a primitive roller coaster that moved riders down a steep track and around curves, with the track ending in water), and, naturally, ice cream and lemonade.

One of the earliest commercial ventures on the oceanfront was Sandborn's Pavilion, a series of concessions and bathhouses housed in the 10th Avenue Pavilion. Gordon's was another popular pavilion. Like other resorts on the Shore, Belmar had beachfront photographic studios, dance halls, bandstands, and the ever-popular bowling alley. As fishing and crabbing were so

The purchase of stately buildings constructed for the 1876 Centennial Exposition in nearby Philadelphia enhanced several Jersey Shore resorts. Ocean Beach (later called Belmar) acquired six such structures, including one that was reassembled as the Colorado House, pictured here alongside the town's first boardwalk.

popular, the riverfront gave the beach some competition for amusements. In one such establishment, known as Captain Kidd's Pavilion and Boathouse, the selection of amusements included a hand-carved carousel.

Belmar's Signature

In the late 1920s Belmar felt pressured by competing seaside communities to build a unique, signature resort facility. Spring Lake to the south had just completed an impressive saltwater pool facility and was in the planning stages of a second pool pavilion. The well-established giants along the coast, Atlantic City and Asbury Park, had also recently completed stately beach-

front public halls. The Historic American Buildings Survey engineering records note that "Belmar's small size did not diminish the municipal pride at stake in the city's beachfront architecture."

The *New York Times*, in an April 1929 article with the banner headline "New Asbury Casino Ready This Summer," noted how Belmar "is emerging in an ambitious program of municipal improvements, including the paving of three streets leading to the beach. A new $15,000 pavilion will be erected and the Belmar Fishing Club has announced plans for a new clubhouse." Fishing, both commercial and recreational, had been a traditional, popular activity at Belmar (especially with the resort's proximity to the Shark River), so the addition

Above: By the early twentieth century, the Belmar walkway was lined with hotels, boarding houses, and cottages. This is a view from the fishing pier looking south.

Below: Gordon's Pavilion was a popular spot on the Belmar boardwalk at the turn of the century. Pavilions provided a comfortable escape from the heat, where visitors could take advantage of the refreshing sea breeze in the pre–air-conditioning era. Most also provided bathhouses and concession stands.

of a handsome fishing pier seemed logical. The land for the pier was originally purchased in 1881 by the Ocean Beach Association, which sold the site to the Shark River Company, which then leased it to the Ocean Pier Company to construct a fishing pier and two-story building. The Ocean Pier Company later bought the pier from the Shark River group, leased it, experienced financial difficulty, and eventually lost control of the pier and property to its tenant, the Belmar Fishing Club. In 1929 the club decided to replace the old wooden structure, and construction began on September 21. After much bickering over what type and style of building to construct, the club and town chose Spanish Mission, the architectural style fashionable along the Jersey Shore in the 1920s and 1930s. Many likened the new establishment to the Music Pier that had been recently completed in Ocean City. Although the club was and still is private, the community took great pride in its new signature building. Because the original pier owners had permitted important community events to take place on the pier, it was assumed that the Belmar Fishing Club would afford the borough the same privilege.

Belmar's beach benefited from the early-twentieth-century practice of building jetties to protect valuable inlets. In Belmar's case, a jetty constructed to protect the Shark River inlet disturbed the natural northward-flowing sand and starved Avon-by-the-Sea and Bradley Beach on the north side of the jetty. Meanwhile, on the south side, Belmar's oceanfront grew to enviable proportions. Like some of its northern neighbors, Belmar was close enough to Asbury Park and Long Branch that there was little motivation to build sizable, expensive boardwalk amusement centers.

After the Storms

Belmar slid comfortably into the role of a family-oriented, quiet resort town, capitalizing on its assets: the Shark River marina and, naturally, the boardwalk and beautiful, expansive beach. The river resembles a large lake and is frequented by small boats. Of course, Belmar, along with its neighboring resorts, has been battered from time to time by hurricanes and northeasters that either partially or completely destroyed its boardwalk. And just like the other villages along the coastline, the town would rebuild after each event. In 1938, when 30-foot-high seas ruined boardwalks and pavilions along the coast, a local newspaper reported on Belmar, "Half of the boardwalk was removed by the storm, including parts of a new

section which was being rebuilt under the WPA [Works Progress Administration]. The estimated damage is $100,000." The following year two large jetties were built to protect the section of beach that was lost in the storm. The cost was $200,000 for both the jetties and the new boardwalk. The town officials also took the opportunity to widen the walkway as well as Ocean Boulevard.

The 1944 Great Atlantic Hurricane and the Great Atlantic Storm of 1962 continued the onslaught on the fragile Belmar beachfront. In 1992 a savage winter northeaster did more damage along the coastline than many hurricanes in the past. The three-day event beginning on Friday, December 11, was the most powerful storm to hit the coast in three decades. In a full-page map and directory listing all of the resorts and their damage, the *New York Times* described Belmar's plight as "severe damage to four-mile boardwalk; beach erosion."

Belmar took a unique approach to the problem after the storm: Town officials chose to make a ¼-mile section of the boardwalk—17th to 20th Avenues—removable. In an interview with the *Times* in 1997, Mayor Kenneth E. Pringle said, "This stuff is expensive, but we couldn't do away with the boardwalk, which attracts so many tourists." He added, "I guess we accepted the realities of Mother Nature and made a strategic withdrawal. It's what I like to call peace with honor."

The resort had estimated that even during calm winters and hurricane seasons, the city was spending approximately $60,000 a year for just plain vanilla–type timber replacement and renailing. Instead of rebuilding a section at a time, Pringle decided to go the portable route. At the end of each season, forklifts removed the portable sections and stacked the walkway six blocks from the ocean in a municipal parking lot. Taking the boardwalk down became a local tradition, and crowds gathered to watch their summer playground move to safer grounds. Pringle planned on constructing a permanent boardwalk when the beach replenishment became a reality, and by 2000 the strand was rebuilt and so was the year-round boardwalk. The 1992 storm convinced some towns to rebuild with synthetic material, but Belmar stayed with

The Belmar boardwalk in 1925, four years after an 80-mile-per-hour gale turned it into a pile of kindling in May 1921. Boardwalks represented a major source of income for Jersey Shore resorts, so towns along the coast had a vested interest in rebuilding immediately after a destructive storm.

The September hurricane of 1938 brought 30-foot-high seas, tearing the Belmar boardwalk to shreds and tossing sections of it hundreds of feet inland.

The 1938 hurricane damage from 16th to 17th Avenues. The couple on the right is standing on a section of the walkway that the summer before was the pathway for thousands of tourists.

wood. Pringle told the *Times* that "what you make a stationary boardwalk out of was sort of like a debate over the material you use to make the deck chairs on the *Titanic*."

Public Access

In the late 1980s, access to the beach became an issue with some Jersey Shore towns and especially Belmar, when the New Jersey State public advocate sued several resorts, charging that they were using excessive beach fees to limit access to their beach. All of the towns involved settled expect Belmar, which went to trial and lost the landmark case. The ruling, known as *Sutton v. Borough of Belmar*, held that shore resorts do not own their beaches, but rather hold them in trust for the residents of New Jersey. The judge found that the fees Belmar was charging exceeded the town's real costs, both direct and indirect, in operating the beach. In other words, the money was being used for other purposes. He ordered Belmar to create a separate accounting system for all of its beach revenues and expenditures so the cash flow could be monitored. At the time the borough administrators refused to comply

with the determination of the court, until a court order forced their hand. The mayor took a hard line and promised to close the beaches before lowering the daily beach fee from $8.00 a day to $3.25, as ordered by the courts. Local attorney Ken Pringle, with the backing of the Belmar Chamber of Commerce, launched a recall campaign, and the mayor and one commissioner were removed from office. Pringle became mayor, and the residents of Belmar voted in the Small Municipality Plan to change their form of government from a three-person commission to a directly elected mayor.

In the end the court ruling benefited the Belmar boardwalk. Until the ruling a part of the revenue from beach fees was used to help keep property taxes as low as possible. Many advocates felt that borough officials were squeezing money from the beach to funnel into other operations, thus inflating the beach's actual direct and indirect costs. Once the decision was finalized by the public advocate, the borough began using the beach resources to improve the boardwalk. Belmar is free to raise beach fees, with the caveat that the money is spent on the boardwalk and beachfront.

The Belmar Fishing Club was the pride of Belmar. It was constructed in 1929 in the Spanish Mission style then fashionable along the Jersey Shore.

Polishing Its Image

Over the last decade, Belmar has been waging a different type of battle—to reclaim the resort as a haven for family tourists and full-time residents. The town's reputation as a loud, rowdy summer hangout for twenty-something groups of people who "kick in" to rent houses began in the 1970s, when the real estate market became depressed and speculators picked up broken down, oversized older homes for little money.

So tarnished was the borough's image that in November 2004, a majority of the residents of tiny South Belmar voted to change their town's name to Lake Como (in reference to the small body of water separating South Belmar from fashionable Spring Lake) to distance themselves from their rowdy neighbor to the north. They hoped that by returning to their roots (the region was known as Como at the turn of the twentieth century), real estate values would increase, and Lake Como would become more of a tony, Spring Lake–style community.

While the mayor of Belmar wished his neighbor well, he and his community have also felt the sting of their borough's tumultuous reputation. In 1992 an MTV Sports Festival concert pulled 150,000 people into the tiny seaside village to hear a popular rap group. It ended up in a full-scale riot, with neighboring police forces called in to help the Belmar police establish order. Twenty-eight people were arrested, and almost forty were injured. Mayor Pringle himself was struck in the head with a bottle as he attempted to direct traffic. Newspaper reports claimed the incident could be characterized as a racial disturbance. Four weeks later, in anticipation of a large gathering of African-American students on the beach, an army of state troopers and police from adjoining towns flooded the seaside resort. This annual event began with a picnic in Philadelphia involving eight national African-American fraternities and sororities

Above: Today the Belmar boardwalk is predominately noncommercial and amusement-free, with only a few pavilions and concession stands along the beach.

Right: Ocean Beach was created in 1872 when forty-one pioneers formed an association and subdivided their land into 161 lots. The massive Columbia Hotel, illustrated here, was the pride of the new community.

that included as many as 125,000 people. A group of the students had begun a tradition in the early 1980s of traveling to Belmar the day after the picnic. The borough officials and state troopers claimed they were only there to maintain order after the MTV incident, but the students felt the heavy-handed approach was racially motivated. Although representatives of the National Association for the Advancement of Colored People who attended the event thought the police presence was intimidating, Mayor Pringle told the *Times*, "You're not going to hear me apologize for a large police presence. We're going to keep the peace, period."

The borough's attempt to tone down Belmar's reputation and bring back families began in the late 1980s, when they began to close the bars earlier than usual. In the summer of 1986, half of the 12,000 calls made to police between Memorial Day and Labor Day involved minor complaints, including excessive noise. At that time Belmar had eighteen bars, with a full-time population of just over 3,000 citizens. Residents complained to their elected officials as they watched their property values decline and their backyards fill up with empty beer bottles.

The Pringle administration decided to push back. Belmar had become a northern version of Fort Lauderdale, Florida, and, just as its southern neighbor had shed the spring break moniker, so would Belmar. In 2004 the full-time population of just over 7,000 residents would swell to over 70,000 on steamy, summer weekends. These were valuable tourist dollars that the borough needed, but the "Animal House" tone of the resort had to change.

Mayor Pringle turned to strict enforcement of the town's laws to send a clear message to the resort's younger visitors. The law was modeled on a New Jersey statute that permitted municipalities to bring uncaring "bad neighbor" landlords to justice. If their tenants committed two "quality of life" violations in a twelve-month period—such as fighting, excessive noise, or even public urination—the city could move against the property owner and obtain a $5,000 bond to cover enforcement costs. If next-door neighbors complained about a property, Belmar's Dawn Patrol paid the offending residence an early morning call—not fun after a night of barhopping—and counted heads. If a third offense took place after the posting of the bond, Belmar placed a county sheriff outside the residence, and the landlord was forced to pick up his or her cost. Pringle let everyone know it was not business as usual.

A 1938 aerial view of Belmar from the Spring Lake Gate looking north. By this period the jetty built to protect the Shark River inlet had starved the neighboring resorts to the north of valuable sand, while building up the Belmar strand. This photo was taken just weeks before a vicious hurricane destroyed the beachfront.

In a recent edition of a local paper, Mayor Pringle replied to a letter from a young man who accused Belmar of harassing renters and implied that the resort could not survive without them. The irate author added that if residents of the borough wanted a family environment, they should move elsewhere. Pringle pointed out that the tide had turned and noted, "Years of zero-tolerance policing, heavy fines, tougher enforcement of our housing and property maintenance codes . . . and aggressive enforcement of the 'animal house' laws are sending the message to tenants and landlords that this is not their father's Belmar." The no-nonsense mayor reminded the public that his city will always welcome tourists, but like any host, "our residents get to set the terms of the invitation we extend." He concluded with the borough's new caveat: "Respect our residents' quality of life, or be prepared to get a swift kick in the wallet. Anyone who has a problem with that should find another place to spend their summers."

His approach seems to be working. Aided by a robust real estate market, the number of summer rental units has dropped from 1,000 a dozen years ago to 300 in 2004. The medium home sale price increased by 30 percent in 2004, a trend that began five years earlier as Jersey Shore property skyrocketed in value. Landlords are taking advantage of the pricey market and selling their properties for huge sums while ridding themselves of the borough's strictly enforced regulations. Most of the rental properties are in such poor condition that they are usually razed by families seeking a cottage by the sea. Some of the bars have disappeared, also victims of rising property values. That is fine with the mayor. Million-dollar homes now stand where college students were dancing on bar tops not too long ago. Because of the public advocate's ruling in the late 1980s case, the more than $2 million raised by selling beach tags in 2004 has been used to improve the boardwalk and attract new families to the resort.

Aggressive redevelopment plans are slated for the inland commercial sector, the Seaport area near the Shark River inlet, and the Belmar marina. Belmar has engineered its master plan to keep the oceanfront sector and boardwalk as uncluttered as possible, and with few exceptions, single-family residential. All this is aimed at reclaiming Belmar as a family resort. As the borough's Web site admits, "After losing direction for a time, Belmar has reclaimed its identity as a strong family-oriented destination during the summer months."

Spring Lake

Spring Lake can claim the longest noncommercial boardwalk on the Jersey Shore. As a reporter noted in 1913: "Spring Lake has generally been content to furnish hotels, cottages, and bathing pavilions, and allow the people to furnish their own facilities for amusement…they are so accustomed to the condition that they rather like it."

A summer day in the early 1920s on the Spring Lake beach. The original South Pavilion is on the left, with the dome of the New Monmouth Hotel visible behind it.

During the summer of 1916, Americans were in the twilight of their age of innocence. They read daily of the staggering numbers of lives lost—both military and civilian—across war-torn Europe. Most realized that, although the United States maintained neutrality, it would only be a matter of time before America would be forced to choose sides in the Great War.

It was a typical summer season at the Jersey Shore, and the hotels were filled with vacationers attempting to escape the rising mercury back home. They kept their mind off the war by discussing more joyous events, such as the first Rose Bowl football game, played on New Year's Day between Brown and Washington State, or the first mass-marketed home refrigerator that sold in 1916 for a whopping $900, the price of a family automobile. The war was an ocean away, and what could be better than a brisk swim off the Jersey beach? As the record crowds enjoyed the refreshing surf and beautiful July weather in the tony resort of Spring Lake, none were aware of the events about to unfold that would forever end a different type of innocence along the shore.

One of the 1876 Centennial Exposition buildings was purchased on December 1, 1876, by John and James Hunter and moved from Philadelphia to Spring Lake. The former Department of Public Comfort Building, used at the world's fair as an information center, was modified to become the famous Lake House. The original building had three wings, but when transformed into the hotel, two wings were joined and one was converted into a bowling alley. Lake House was located at the head of Spring Lake about 100 yards from the railroad depot. It had a commanding view of the ocean and operated until 1904. Potter Park is now where the hotel once stood.

Although legends of shark attacks along the New York and New Jersey coastline had long existed, in 1916 many experts believed that they were just that—legends. Even the $500 prize offered in 1891 by the shipping mogul Hermann Oelrichs for an authenticated incident of a person being attacked by a shark north of Cape Hatteras, North Carolina, remained unclaimed. That was about to change.

The first attack took place over the Fourth of July weekend, in just 3½ feet of water off the coast of Beach Haven, 50 miles south of Spring Lake. The victim was a thirty-year-old University of Pennsylvania graduate. The son of a physician, Charles E. Vansant had been enjoying a swim in the cooling surf of the Atlantic with his beloved golden retriever when he was attacked. Sun worshippers on the beach noticed the shark's fin and screamed to warn the young man, but it was too late. Within a matter of seconds Vansant was fatally wounded by the shark's powerful jaws. Although a heroic lifeguard fought and won a tug-of-war with the beast over the stricken swimmer, Vansant died from shock and loss of blood an hour after being brought to shore.

The incident was considered an anomaly by the officials and scientific "experts," following the conventional wisdom of the era. The *New York Times* described Vansant's death with no mention of a man-eating shark, so bathers along the shore paid little attention to the

A view of the Spring Lake boardwalk in 1905 at the time the borough took over the walkway. A resort's first boardwalk was most often composed of planks, which were then taken up at the end of the season. At this early date there were no concessions or amusements along the walkway.

The first pavilions along the Spring Lake boardwalk were small open-air structures on the inland side of the walk. Benches were provided for visitors to rest and take in the view.

This structure, located just south of the New Monmouth Hotel, provided a pleasant venue to meet with friends, hold a concert, or just escape from the heat to enjoy lunch. The dome of the hotel can be seen on the far left of the photograph.

Above: The first South End Pavilion was privately owned and was, as noted in the Library of Congress' Historic American Buildings Survey, "constructed with large Stick Style brackets and balustraded flat roof that doubled as an observation platform." The open galley below the observation deck provided a view of the saltwater pool inside the building. On the boardwalk a shaded concession stand created an inviting place to stop for a souvenir.

Below: A citizens group constructed a series of open sun shelters for children on the beach. One can be seen on the right side of this image.

story. That would change just five days later in Spring Lake.

Charles Bruder, a popular Swiss-born Spring Lake hotel bell captain, became the hungry shark's second victim as he swam just a thousand feet from shore. Friends reported later that seconds after Bruder ventured out a bit farther from their group of swimmers, he was heard to scream, "A shark bit me . . . he bit my legs off!" Those were his final words. When several onlookers commandeered a rowboat and dragged poor Bruder onto the boat, they saw both his feet were indeed missing. He died almost immediately of massive blood loss. The shark was nowhere to be seen.

That incident raised the first coastwide shark alert in the history of the country. Mesh barriers appeared up and down the Jersey Shore, and special shark units patrolled the waters along the coastline. Oddly, some experts would still not believe that a shark was preying on humans. As the *Times* wrote, "It was suggested that a huge mackerel had killed the bather and not a shark." No matter. Whether it was a great white shark or a mackerel on steroids, the carefree summer was over.

From Farmland to Fashionable Resort

The resort of Spring Lake, south of Belmar, is an upper-middle-class town once referred to as the "Irish Riviera." The town featured three bodies of water: Wreck Pond, Lake Como (formerly Three-Cornered Pond), and Spring Lake, a crystal-clear, spring-fed lake (formerly Fresh Creek Pond). Just forty years before the great white shark incident, these were surrounded by quiet farms. By the time of the attacks, Spring Lake was considered one of the most fashionable resorts on the Jersey Shore.

The development of the farmland followed the traditional formula of many fledgling resorts. Land would be acquired, and a grand structure—later transformed to a hotel—was built to accommodate potential land buyers. An official "Land Improvement Company" would be organized and the farmland subdivided into lots, followed by the construction of streets, avenues, and eventually cottages. The holy grail of any new resort was the treasured railroad connection—the lifeline to the hoards of eager vacationers and their money. In the 1870s and

The saltwater pool and the entrance to the bathhouses at the North End Pavilion. Lockers can be seen in the background.

The original North End Pavilion was almost a twin of the South End Pavilion, complete with gallery and saltwater pool. By 1907 the Borough of Spring Lake had taken over the North Pavilion. That there are no concession stands outside the building reflects the resort's reserved atmosphere.

1880s, the railroad finally reached southern Monmouth County.

By the late nineteenth century, four seaside farms located between Wreck Pond and Lake Como were developed into four distinct seaside enclaves by a variety of entrepreneurs. The communities were called Spring Lake Beach, Villa Park, Brighton, and Como. Como achieved an aura of exclusiveness from its inception by requiring that cottages be built on 100-by-50-foot lots at a minimum cost of $3,000. That was a lot of money in the late nineteenth century, so only the privileged could afford to build Como "cottages." Brighton officials banked on the popular temperance movement as a way to ensure peace and quiet by the sea, writing alcohol restrictions into their deeds. By 1903 the four neighboring communities had come together to form the famous resort of Spring Lake.

Developers erected grand hotels along with "summer cottages" that matched them in size and grandeur. One such developer, the Lake House Company, was organized in 1875, and in 1876 the behemoth, four-story

Monmouth House was completed. The hotel was the height of elegance, with 270 bedrooms, a dining room, and all the modern amenities, including a steam-powered elevator and "electric calls" in each room. The front of the hotel looked onto the Atlantic Ocean. The western facade faced the formal Victorian gardens around the popular spring-fed lake, the namesake of the borough. The hotel was designed by Stephen Decatur Button, an architect best known for his work in Cape May. A contemporary account described its location as "midway between the ocean and the lake, 200 yards from each, this hotel served as a nucleus for the growing settlement of summer residents, and in its immediate neighborhood are streets, cottages and churches, forming a resort conspicuous for the elegance of its exterior." Monmouth House also provided its guests with a fenced-in private beach and the town's first "boardwalk," a wooden walkway connecting the hotel to the beachfront. A two-story pavilion on the walkway offered hotel guests a retreat from the sun. The spring-fed lake was a center of attention, with a plank and asphalt walkway installed along its shore. A description of the site in 1889 noted that "a rustic bridge spans its west end." The

The namesake of Pier Beach belonged to the Rod and Gun Club, organized in the late nineteenth century. The pier was razed after years of battling King Neptune.

lake was so clean that apparently a coin dropped to a depth of 25 feet could be easily located and identified from a rowboat.

"Centennial Relics"

The close of the country's 1876 Centennial Exposition, held in Philadelphia, gave nearby towns the chance to buy the beautiful buildings at a reasonable cost. Lumber was much more expensive than labor in 1876, and improved rail service permitted these monstrous "Centennial relics" to be disassembled and moved to new locations. Spring Lake acquired four structures: the Department of Public Comfort Building, the Missouri State Building, the Portuguese Government Pavilion, and the New Hampshire State Building.

The Public Comfort Building—transported, reerected, and remodeled—opened as the Lake House on June 9,

1877. This successful hotel operated with a "family theme" until it was demolished in 1904. Lumber from the monstrous Centennial Agricultural Hall was used for various projects in Spring Lake, including a bridge over the Wreck Pond inlet and the construction of numerous cottages. The town's sole remaining Centennial building, the former Missouri State Pavilion, is today a private residence located at 411 Ocean Road. In 1898 another landmark, the Bath and Tennis Club, was constructed on New Jersey Avenue and later became known as the Casino. It was the social venue for the society of Spring Lake and offered a variety of events from concerts to world-class tennis matches. Its property consisted of seventeen lots—the building covering seven, with the other ten lots reserved for ten tennis courts. During its long history, the club hosted national tennis stars such as Vic Seixus and Don Bugge. Interestingly, in 1913 the *New York Times* noted that the Casino was the location of a "monster rally of the forces of the antisuffrage." The *Times* article goes on to mention that "Spring Lake is the Summer capital of the movement in New Jersey because so many of the Trenton women who are active in the matter make their homes here in the heated term."

On the morning of September 19, 1900, the scourge of every wooden city by the sea struck Spring Lake. A fire

broke out shortly after midnight, and it was not satisfied until it consumed the resort's three grandest hotels. Lost were the Monmouth House, the Carleton Hotel, and the Essex Hotel, along with the town's commercial district. In 1903 the New Monmouth Hotel was constructed on the grounds of the original Monmouth of a larger scale than its namesake. The hotel was a favorite of vacationers and lasted until 1974. In 1909 another conflagration claimed the Breakers, one of the largest hotels on the Jersey coast (not to be confused with the current Breakers hotel and banquet facility, formerly known as the Wilburton-by-the-Sea). It was only by luck that the fire did not spread to the New Monmouth. After the fires, two stately cottages were renamed "Essex" and "Sussex" and moved to the north side of Essex Avenue to become part of the new Essex and Sussex Hotel, built in 1914. Today the historic hotel offers luxury oceanfront condominiums for senior citizens.

A Step Back to the Past

Spring Lake can claim to have the longest noncommercial boardwalk on the New Jersey coast. In 1913 the *New York Times* described the resort's reserved atmosphere in an article discussing the events planned for the Fourth of July weekend. Although a round of dances and social

Above: A busy summer day in 1947 when the Spring Lake boardwalk was still a traditional wooden walkway. The Essex and Sussex Hotel seen in the background dominates the oceanfront.

Below: When this photograph was taken, the residents of the Essex and Sussex Hotel could enjoy the hotel's private beach. The beach is fenced off and a private walkway led from the hotel to the beach.

Inset: A view of the Essex and Sussex Hotel, which appeared in the 1981 film *Ragtime*. The hotel has since been renovated for condominiums.

events were planned, there was an absence of fireworks and no water carnival on the lake. As the reporter noted, "Spring Lake has generally been content to furnish hotels, cottages, and bathing pavilions, and allow the people to furnish their own facilities for amusement, and they are so accustomed to the condition that they rather like it."

One traditional celebration—Salt Water Day, or Big Sea Day—still takes place on the second Saturday of August. No one knows the reason why that particular date was chosen, but records indicate that Big Sea Day began in the late eighteenth century when the area was a collection of remote farms. The farmers would dress up in their "go to meeting" clothes, hitch their horses to the family wagon or carriage, and head for the Atlantic Ocean. Thousands of people attended the annual event—

a sort of seaside hoedown—to renew old acquaintances and enjoy the refreshing surf.

The resort's walkway was privately maintained from the 1880s until the borough took it over in 1904. A photograph taken the next year shows it as a series of boards laid horizontally along the beachfront. Small pavilions with benches dotted the inland side of the boardwalk. Eventually the boardwalk was elevated, with wooden stairways leading to the sand and a extending over the beach just across and south of the Monmouth Hotel site. In addition, the Rod and Gun Club established a fishing pier that extended far enough out over the surf to give anglers the impression that they were out to sea during high tide. The area where it stood is still known as Pier Beach, although years of northeasters, hurricanes, and fires eventually forced the razing of that structure.

Above: In this circa 1918 view, lights have been installed along the boardwalk, and the pavilions are now enclosed should a sudden thunderstorm appear on the horizon.

Right: A 1940s post card of the current South End Pavilion pool. A note on the back of the card reads: "You would love this pool of ocean water. The high dive is a bit too high for me, but affords a lot of entertainment as there are some swell divers here."

The Spring Lake boardwalk is anchored at the north and south ends by two distinctive buildings. Originally open pavilions constructed with large Stick-Style brackets and flat roofs that doubled as observation platforms, by 1926 they had outlived their usefulness and were regarded by the wealthier residents as not contemporary enough for their upscale resort. The mayor at the time described the buildings as "antiquated, too small and far from being . . . ornament(s) to our beautiful beachfront." He added that they received "much unfavorable criticism from our summer guests." In the fall of 1926, the mayor and council commissioned plans for two new bathing pavilions from designer E. H. Schmeider, the Spring Lake borough architect and engineer. Schmeider's plans for two bathing pavilions were immediately approved, the construction to be financed by a $250,000 bond issue. The South End Pavilion was completed in 1929 and the North End in 1931, garnering praise from a contemporary newspaper: "This attractive, substantially constructed group recently completed offers bathers every pleasure and convenience under the most ideal conditions."

The South Pavilion is constructed of masonry, with green glazed terra-cotta tiles depicting lobsters, frogs, crabs, and willows in an art deco style. Bathhouses and a saltwater pool were provided for the residents. The North End Pavilion, located on the boardwalk at 5th and Warren Avenues, also had a lovely saltwater pool and bathhouses. The terra-cotta tiles here represent a variety of subjects, including a bird in flight, a lighthouse, a leaping fish, a sailboat, and a pelican grasping a frog. Both pavilions offered an open observation deck and a small concession area. Some remodeling has taken place over the years, including railing changes and the replacement of the tar roofs on the bathhouses with plastic roofing.

During the period in which these pavilions were built, Spring Lake officials set in place zoning ordinances to guarantee the noncommercial aspect of the boardwalk. Among the prohibitions cited were "carousels, roller coasters, whirligigs, merry-go-rounds, Ferris wheels or similar amusement devices." It is interesting that the borough made such a large financial commitment to build—$250,000 in 1920s money—while at the same time sealing the boardwalk's fate as a noncommercial entity.

The Spring Lake boardwalk today is composed almost completely of recycled plastic. The 1.8-mile commercial walkway is a
favorite among joggers and those seeking a peaceful seaside
promenade.

Today, with the exception of the North and South End Pavilions, the Spring Lake boardwalk is completely non-commercial: no rides, no games of chance, no cotton candy or funnel cake—and the residents love it just that way. As with Cape May to the south, residents feel that visitors come and stay at their resort for the ambience, the collection of Victorian homes and bed-and-breakfasts, and to take a step back to the past. There is always the quick ride to Wildwood, Point Pleasant, or Seaside if the family needs a dose of traditional Jersey Shore board-walk fare.

Point Pleasant

By 1925 Point Pleasant had a permanent 2-mile-long wood boardwalk. Shortly thereafter, the enterprising Charles Jenkinson built an open-air pavilion that ultimately included concessions, a bandstand, and a sizable dance hall. It was the beginning of Jenkinson's eventual domination of the Point Pleasant boardwalk.

While boardwalk midways have always been a fascination for children, nothing can compete with being on a fine Jersey Shore beach itself, with a pail and shovel. Here children on the Point Pleasant beach engage in the age-old challenge, "How deep can we dig?"

November 1918 was a time of joy for the United States and Europe. On the eleventh hour of the eleventh day of the eleventh month—November 11, 1918—the armistice became official, ending the almost incalculable carnage known as the Great War. The popular songs that year were "Till We Meet Again" and "K-K-K-Katy," and they could be heard in every dancehall in every city and hamlet as the country desperately sought a return to normalcy.

That same winter Eugene O'Neill, the man who was to become the only American playwright ever to receive the Nobel Prize for literature, was seeking an inexpensive place convenient to New York City where he could live while he was supervising the production of his play, *Where the Cross Is Mad*. Money was tight, and the yet-to-become-famous author was relying on an allowance provided by his father and the meager earnings from his first productions. O'Neill chose Point Pleasant, knowing that the summer crowds were hibernating until the following May. He believed the deserted beachfront community would be the perfect environment to work on new material. It is believed that O'Neill wrote *Chris Christopherson* during his stay in New Jersey, a play that would eventually evolve into *Anna Christie*.

In 1992 Jenkinson's introduced the Flitzer to the boardwalk. The 1,000-foot-long, high-tech thrill machine is a steel-track roller coaster that looms 25 harrowing feet above the walkway.

By all accounts O'Neill was not enamored with the Jersey Shore during that winter. His wife, Agnes Boulton, wrote: "There was nothing in that flat New Jersey landscape he could identify with any part of his own personality." She added, "Even the ocean appeared uninteresting to him, with its waves breaking monotonously on the sand close to the old woode[n] boardwalk."

Although the shore was not to O'Neill's taste, the Boulton family had deep roots in the region, where they had owned a circa 1865 modest two-story, wood-frame home they referred to as the Old House. In 1927, when Agnes and Eugene divorced, she moved with their children, Shane and Oona, back to Point Pleasant. Oona was beloved by the locals and grew into a stunningly beautiful woman. She made headlines when, at the age of eighteen, she married fifty-four-year-old Charlie Chaplin. The two remained happily married until Chaplin died in 1977.

A Railroad Resort

Most of the visionaries who developed the pre-railroad seashore wilderness knew that once the final spike in the track was hammered, these backwater communities would grow exponentially in value. In many cases, such

Above: The Resort House Bathing Pavilion, built in 1884. This was the beach pavilion for the Resort House hotel, built by the Point Pleasant Land Company, the company that purchased 250 acres of farmland and began developing the resort. A temporary boardwalk was used to keep the sand on the beach and out of the pavilion. Although automobiles are seen in this image, access to the pavilion was originally by horse-drawn trolley.

Left: The Wuest Casino, visible behind the pavilion on the inland side of the boardwalk, was constructed in 1893 and would eventually house a carousel, a traditional Jersey Shore attraction.

Right: A more permanent boardwalk can be seen in the background behind a popular beach pavilion.

The Point Pleasant boardwalk circa 1920. This was the era when, even on such a primitive boardwalk, families dressed in their best to see and be seen.

An early-twentieth-century view of the northern boardwalk, including the Wuest Casino (left), a dapper woman sporting stylish sunglasses sitting on a boardwalk bench, and the fishing pier in the distance on the right.

as in Atlantic City, developers and railroad consortiums together planned the resort, paying pennies for land that would skyrocket in value when the railroad was completed. The consortium would claim their record profits from land sales, and the new cottage owners would provide a steady stream of income for the railroads. It was a win-win situation.

Point Pleasant, like so many other Jersey Shore resorts, came about when the Jersey Central Railroad made the area accessible to trainloads of visitors from New York City. They were persuaded to extend the line to Point Pleasant by its pioneering founder, Captain John Arnold, who offered the railroad money and land. Before this, the only alternative from New York to Point Pleasant was a full-day ride by stagecoach over primitive roads. The resort also became fashionable with Philadelphians using the Philadelphia and Long Branch Railroad. Thus a desolate beachfront, known as Inlet Land for the number of inlets and lakes that exist in the region, developed from a handful of houses scattered throughout the region to a real community in 1899, with four large hotels, five churches, a newspaper, trolley, and even portable boardwalk. Electric lights replaced the whale-oil lanterns and lamps used by the pioneer families in Point Pleasant.

In 1877 the Point Pleasant Land Company purchased the 250-acre Forman Farm, which included the beachfront, and began to develop a city by the sea. One year later, as per the resort development business model, the grand four-story Resort House hotel opened for business on Richmond Avenue. The hotel evolved with the resort and under new ownership was doubled in size in 1895, coinciding with the arrival of the railroad. It now offered more than a hundred rooms, steam heat, elevators, and even indoor plumbing. In that same year, the resort's first mass-transit system, a horse-drawn trolley, began to transport new cottage owners and visitors from the hotel to the beach, where the hotel provided a bathing pavilion. Other hotels began to appear shortly thereafter, notably the Carrollton House, built in 1898.

The Evolving Boardwalk

The boardwalk at Point Pleasant evolved as most others did along the coastline. In 1880 the first pavilion was constructed on the beach at Atlantic Avenue. The year 1884 saw the construction of the Resort House Bathing Pavilion and the addition of a horse-drawn trolley that transported beach lovers to the pavilion. In 1890 a large, temporary plank walkway was constructed, but, as was common at the time, it washed out to sea in 1892. A series of primitive, portable walkways installed between 1892 and 1912 all suffered the same fate. If the boardwalk made it through the summer season, it would be hauled to high ground for the hard northern shore winters. But if a sudden summer buster blew in from the Atlantic, sections of the walkway where once fashionable visitors strolled might end up as driftwood on an island beach. In 1911 the Point Pleasant Improvement Association was formed to work with the borough to plan a new walkway and remove it from the hands of private individuals.

The streets of Point Pleasant took on a festive appearance in 1894 as the electricity that was required to power the first electric trolley line also provided power to several affluent private homeowners. In 1915 the *New York Times* reported, "The municipal authorities during the winter constructed a new boardwalk which is 1,000 feet longer than the old walk. This new walk has been artistically lighted at night."

By 1925 Point Pleasant Beach had a permanent boardwalk that extended from the Manasquan Inlet south for approximately 2 miles. Shortly thereafter Charles Jenkinson acquired a section of beachfront property along the boardwalk and began construction. Jenkinson was no stranger to boardwalk resorts, having previously operated concessions in both Asbury Park and Ocean Grove. His Point Pleasant pavilion officially opened on July 7, 1928, and his name eventually became synonymous with the Point Pleasant boardwalk.

The enterprising promoter built an open-air structure on the beach, complete with the usual concessions for sun lovers, including a soda shop and a candy counter. In a bold step, across from his open-air pavilion, he invested in what was advertised as the largest saltwater swimming pool between Asbury Park and Atlantic City. That first pavilion also provided a bandstand for concerts, a popular seaside attraction of the day. Jenkinson's Pavilion was so successful that he enlarged and enclosed

A 1908 view of the Point Pleasant boardwalk. Owned and maintained by private individuals, the movable walkway was stored away at the end of the season. Though the borough, as early as 1896, leased sections of the boardwalk, it did not assume responsibility for the evolving thoroughfare until the first permanent structure was completed in 1915.

Risden's Casino, a Point Pleasant landmark for over half a century, can be seen in the upper right of this image. An unnamed hurricane in 1938 caused more damage to the Point Pleasant boardwalk than any other storm in the resort's recorded history. Risden's Casino was severely damaged along with 3,800 feet of the walkway. As a reminder of a past way of life, bathhouse facilities are still in operation today at what is known as Risden's Beach.

it the next year, including a monstrous dance hall complete with a 2,000-square-foot dance floor. Despite the worries of the Great Depression, which pushed many amusement operators to the brink of extinction, Jenkinson's Pavilion continued to expand, even adding a miniature golf course. Charles Jenkinson acquired additional assets in 1934, including more beachfront property, bathhouses, and a competitor's pavilion. (As of 2004 the borough only owns 300 feet of beachfront property; the rest belongs to private operators such as Jenkinson, Martell, and Joseph Risden.)

In the midst of this success, a horrific hurricane on September 21, 1938, raised havoc in the tiny community; indeed, many historians believe it to be the worst storm in recorded history to hit the Point Pleasant Beach community. It rearranged the boardwalk, ripping 3,800 feet of it to shreds, along with the electric lights that lined the walkway. The section of the Point Pleasant boardwalk south to Bay Head was destroyed and has never been replaced; as of this printing, the boardwalk ends at New Jersey Avenue. The unnamed hurricane also destroyed a major section of the Point Pleasant fishing pier and inflicted heavy damage on the Atlantic Baths and Risden's Casino. The traffic on Ocean Avenue was halted as large sections of the boardwalk, along with concession stands, were swept onto the roadway.

A curiosity of the Point Pleasant boardwalk revolves around its northern section. Unlike the commercial boardwalks of Ocean City or Wildwood—which pack amusements and concessions onto every possible piece of lumber—or the noncommercial walks of Ocean Grove and Spring Lake, the Point Pleasant walkway is a delightful hybrid. While the southern end contains one of the most popular amusement centers on the Jersey Shore, the boardwalk's northern end passes a quaint community of summer cottages and bungalows that began as a tent village. Today one local favorite is referred to as the Frank Sinatra House, not because he lived here but because its owners have an affinity for Old Blue Eyes and often serenade walkers with his music.

This view, looking south, captures a permanent, busy Point Pleasant boardwalk during the height of the 1937 season. Was the automobile in the shed a new model on display or was it a raffle prize?

A section of Jenkinson's original pavilion can be seen to the left of the fishing pier. Originally built as an open structure, the facility provided a dance hall and bandstand, as well as miscellaneous concessions. A large saltwater pool was constructed across from the pavilion. This was the beginning of Charles Jenkinson's eventual domination of the Point Pleasant boardwalk.

By 1947 Jenkinson's Pavilion had become a landmark on the walkway. After his father's death in 1937, Orlo Jenkinson took over the business and, with each new season, came additional acquisitions and expansions. In 1940 the younger Jenkinson christened the miniature beach train that connected his beachfront amusement centers. A typical summer day would consist of a ride on the beach train, a famous Jenkinson's hamburger and a birch beer, then on to the go-Karts, Toboggan, and arcade games.

Building on the Past

Neither the 1938 hurricane nor the passing of founder Charles Jenkinson in 1937 slowed the Jenkinson board-walk juggernaut. The amusement center continued to expand after Charles's son, Orlo, took control of the business. In 1940 another Jenkinson tradition was established: a miniature train. Many a boardwalk memory centers on this little train that until the late 1990s ran along the beach, connecting the original Jenkinson's and a new property near the inlet.

When Orlo Jenkinson died in 1964, his son took over control of the company but sold it in 1977. Its new owner, Pat Storino, immediately began renovating the older facilities. He also acquired competitors Fun Fair and Holiday Playland (renamed Jenkinson's South), which had a genuine hand-carved Dentzel carousel, and later Herman's Amusements. With these purchases, he gained control of most of the commercial boardwalk property. Then on November 22, 1989, a fire destroyed the historic Jenkinson's Pavilion structure that had started it all back in 1928. A late November snowstorm added a surreal look to the seaside scene as firefighters valiantly fought the blaze, and hundreds of bystanders, many in tears, watched the old landmark turn to ashes.

Its replacement replicated many of the original structure's features and added more. Every amusement operation needs a unique attraction that separates it from the pack, and, for Storino, it was the new Jenkinson's Pavilion, built in 1991. He didn't stop there—in 1992 he added a major roller coaster, the Flitzer, and in 1998 a fun house. Fun houses had been traditional on Jersey boardwalks for years, but many had disappeared. Storino bet—and won—that the public would welcome this homage to the good old days.

Today the company name, Jenkinson's Boardwalk, is the Point Pleasant walkway as far as amusements are concerned. Whereas Belmar and Seaside Heights call in rowdier, younger crowds, Point Pleasant has intention-

Left: The Jenkinson's Beach Train became a Point Pleasant tradition, providing memories for thousands of children and adults until it was retired in the late 1990s. It connected Jenkinson's amusement centers at either end of the beach.

Above: The celebratory Big Sea Day, which began in 1896, has now evolved into the popular Festival of the Sea held every September. The traditional celebration dates back to the Algonquin and Lenni-Lenape tribes, who came out to the shore every August to enjoy the refreshing surf. Big Sea Day, or Wash Day as it was sometimes called, became an annual outing for the early settlers in the region. Up to 10,000 men, women, and children would drive their buggies and wagons from their farms to the beach and spend the day sea bathing and celebrating the fine August weather. The festive occasion disappeared around the turn of the century with the buildup of the beachfront and the introduction of the automobile.

Below: The Big Sea Day parade in Point Pleasant in the 1950s. The Greater Point Pleasant Chamber of Commerce revived the annual event in 1950 and, by 1953, more than 100,000 people traveled to the tiny resort town to participate in the longstanding tradition.

Kiddie rides have always been a favorite family tradition on the Point Pleasant boardwalk.

Today Jenkinson's—"The Family Fun Place"—dominates the boardwalk, offering a variety of annual events for families, a first-class amusement facility, and a year-round aquarium.

ally fashioned itself as "The Family Fun Place," with special events ranging from fireworks to concerts to unique shows for children. Attractions include three miniature-golf courses, thrill and kiddie rides, dining at the pavilion, arcades packed with games of skill and chance, and the fun house. The aquarium is open year-round and is a first-class facility, with a 58,000-gallon tank complete with sharks and stingrays. And there is always the Festival of the Sea held every September, when the crowds are down to a roar, but the weather is still beautiful.

Seaside

The installation of a Gustav Dentzel carousel on the boardwalk in 1916 provided the foundation for the prosperous Seaside-area amusement industry that followed. A ride on the magical animals, accompanied by the unforgettable midway sounds of a roll-operated band organ, created lasting boardwalk memories for generations of summer visitors.

Kiddie rides were, and still are, popular on the Seaside boardwalk.

A man of humble beginnings, J. Stanley Tunney was to play a pivotal role in the development of the Seaside boardwalk, as well as the resort town of Seaside Heights. In the 1920s he opened a small boardwalk restaurant in rented space on a beachfront pier. Times were so tough that Tunney had to supplement his income by "mining" the beachfront looking for change and jewelry lost by sea bathers. One day he arrived at his fledgling restaurant to find the entrance to the pier roped off by city officials—the police informed him that the city had deemed the pier unsafe to conduct business. The tenacious entrepreneur cut the rope, entered his restaurant, and was promptly arrested. His wife then stepped in and was immediately led off to join her husband in his cell. The officials eventually relented and released them, but the event had a long-term impact. The enraged Tunney vowed to challenge the local government and was eventually elected mayor, serving for more than a quarter of a century.

Samba Balloons on Casino Pier.

Not long after his arrest, Tunney was walking along the beachfront when he noticed a large barrel that had washed ashore. He managed to transport it home and bore a hole in it. To his delight, it was full of high-quality Irish whiskey. He sold the barrel of liquid gold for $300 and would later say that it was like manna from heaven, as, at the time he found the barrel, his wife was at the bank withdrawing their last few dollars to keep their boardwalk enterprise afloat. From that day on his life took a prosperous turn—the family kept their boardwalk business and entered the amusement business.

Seaside Amusements

A little more than a decade before Tunney found his lucky barrel, Joseph Vanderslice, realizing that Seaside was a promising resort, traveled from Philadelphia to stake his claim in the amusement business there. The Pennsylvania Railroad had made a significant commitment in 1881 to connect Philadelphia with Seaside Heights via a rail bridge over Barnegat Bay to Toms River. The northern railroads had written the Barnegat

Author's note: The Seaside Park and Seaside Heights boardwalks meet to create one of the busiest and most exciting walkways on the Jersey Shore. The approximately 2-mile-long Seaside Park boardwalk is primarily residential with the exception of Funtown Pier, which straddles the Seaside Park–Seaside Heights border. Both are part of separate municipalities, but for the purposes of this book, I refer to this chapter as Seaside.

On June 9, 1955, fire—the scourge of wooden walkways everywhere—paid a visit to Freeman's Amusements, and in a little more than two hours reduced the carousel and busy pier to memories. A faulty neon sign is believed to have started the fire. Fifty-mile-per-hour ocean winds encouraged the blaze to claim three blocks of boardwalk from Dupont Avenue in Seaside Heights to Stockton Avenue in Seaside Park. The blaze was a crushing blow to the community, but J. Stanley Tunney and his associates began immediately to clear the rubble and rebuild for the next season.

Peninsula off as a Philadelphia stomping ground. (Interestingly, the Pennsylvania Railroad's decision to head north after it landed in Seaside Heights and connect with the New York and Long Branch Railroad was responsible for the isolation of noncommercial Island Beach. Today the 11-mile pristine barrier beach of Island Beach State Park delights those looking for a peaceful seaside experience.)

Joseph Vanderslice also knew that the 1914 opening of the first bridge to span Barnegat Bay would guarantee a steady flow of fellow Philadelphians to the resort. As historian John T. Cunningham wrote in 1958, "The automobile democratized Barnegat Peninsula." Because the bridge connected the mainland directly to Seaside Heights, the resort had an advantage over other towns along the Barnegat Peninsula. It wasn't until 1911 that a rugged road reached south from Point Pleasant to Seaside Heights, so the new bridge was critical to the resort's success. Seaside Park, the sister resort to the south, had been founded by Baptists in 1876 in the hopes of duplicating their Methodist brethrens' camp-meeting experience to the north in Ocean Grove. Though the religious community never took hold, the plan no doubt was responsible for the quiet, residential climate of the Seaside Park boardwalk and community compared to the Heights. Five brothers from the Cummings family in Philadelphia, along with another group of investors comprising the Manhasset Realty Company, took advantage of the transportation links and subdivided Seaside Park into lots. The resort was conveniently located for Philadelphians seeking a cottage by the sea, as the north and south latitudes of the Quaker City's limits paralleled the latitudes of both ends of the Barnegat Peninsula.

Vanderslice's move was a bold one. Although the Seaside Heights council approved a boardwalk plan in 1916, conflicts over rights-of-way caused numerous delays and legal battles. (The walkway was eventually built one section at a time and not completed until 1921.) Vanderslice established his own boardwalk and the Senate Amusement Company in 1915, purchasing an old gasoline-powered carousel and building a wooden pier to support his new enterprise. However, fortune did not follow, and Vanderslice was forced to close after the first season. The following year the carousel and pier were purchased by Frank Freeman, who became a major force on the Seaside boardwalk. Freeman sold the old roundabout and installed a brand-new, electric-powered carousel built by Gustav A. Dentzel in his Philadelphia factory.

These photographs of Freeman's in 1936 show the development that had taken place in just two decades from the first time the carousel began spinning memories for a generation of children. By this time a Ferris wheel and busy Skee-Ball and arcade parlor had been added to the list of attractions. Freeman's also provided bathhouses and a beachfront pavilion.

A Dentzel carousel was a thing of beauty. His carvings and those of Daniel Muller, one of his master woodcarvers, were done in what became known as the Philadelphia style. Dentzel horses were beautifully proportioned, graceful, and known for their lifelike expressions. The master carver chose classic poses for his horses and gave them flowing, gently curved manes. The horses' saddles were embellished with intricate, delicate trappings but no jewels. Though few of his carvers signed their work (at the height of the golden age of the carousel, Dentzel had forty craftsmen producing five to six carousels a year), some were known for their own unique flourishes. For example, Dentzel's Italian master carver, Salvatore Cernigliaro, would often add a beautifully detailed clown adorning the saddle, known as the "Cherni" clown. People rode the magical animals to the midway music of a band organ operated by a player piano–style roll. The organ blended snare drums, cymbals, bass drums, bells, and organ music into the wondrous cacophony that once experienced is never forgotten. In addition, there were brightly colored, intricate paintings at the top of the center casing, along with mirrors reflecting hundreds of brightly colored incandescent lights.

The Seaside Dentzel carousel was the seed out of which grew the Seaside Heights, and Seaside Park, amusement industry. Frank Freeman prospered and added new rides and attractions around his prized carousel, including a fishing pier, skating rink, indoor dance hall, and amusement arcade. Freeman was also a politician and served as mayor of Seaside Heights for one term, 1920–1921. By the 1940s Freeman's amusement center had passed into the control of Frank Freeman's onetime maintenance man, J. Stanley Tunney, who was by then the mayor of Seaside Heights. He had done well for himself since finding that barrel of Irish whiskey in the surf. Under Tunney's management, Freeman's Amusements became a favorite tourist location. Early photographs show a bustling amusement center with Skee-Ball parlors, a Ferris wheel, dance hall, bathhouses, free beach, and numerous concessions. Continued growth and success seemed to be in the cards, especially since Freeman's had a twenty-plus-year head start on the new amusement center at the northern end of the walkway in Seaside Heights.

Rising from the Ashes

No boardwalk gypsy fortune-teller could foresee the misfortune looming around the corner for Mr. Tunney. On June 9, 1955, at 6:00 A.M., just as the resort was shaking off the last of the springtime blues and was preparing to meet the onslaught of tourists, a devastating fire broke out on the boardwalk. (It was later believed to have been started by a faulty neon sign.) The alarm was raised by the watch on the oceanfront Coast Guard tower, and firefighters from both Ocean and Monmouth Counties responded. Mayor Tunney later recalled, "When they woke me, I took one look out the window and I kissed it goodbye." As is common with seaside fires, the conflagration was bolstered by 50-mile-per-hour ocean winds as it swept through three blocks of the boardwalk. The firefighters fought valiantly, but when it was over, in barely two hours, the amusement center from Dupont Avenue in Seaside Heights to Stockton Avenue in Seaside Park was reduced to ashes.

The damage was in the millions of dollars, yet the most devastating blow was the loss of the exquisite Dentzel carousel. No one felt that more than J. Stanley Tunney, and no sooner had the ashes of the fire cooled when the tenacious mayor set off to replace it. He eventually located a carousel for sale in Coney Island and spent $22,000 to purchase it and another $20,000 to transport and install the machine. Tunney also invested hundreds of hours of sweat equity in the carousel, restoring many of the animals himself.

By all accounts the carousel that he found was another classic, built by Marcus C. Illions, who had apprenticed for Dentzel's competitor, Charles I. D. Looff, before establishing his own factory, M. C. Illions and Sons, Carousell [sic] Works, in Coney Island in 1909. Illions's figures had elaborate trappings, including jewels, natural horsehair tails, and metal horseshoes. The machine had a painting of Illions himself on the ornate rounding board. To make his carousel even more unique, Tunney replaced several figures with those created by other master carvers. The machine spun magical memories for thirty-five years until it was dismantled and the figures

In 1932 what had been the sedate northern end of the Seaside boardwalk came to life when Linus Gilbert purchased a carousel that had been damaged in the Island Beach Park fire. It was a "mixed machine" with most of the figures carved by William Dentzel and Charles Looff. Gilbert's carousel predated by five years any other amusements in what would become Casino Pier.

sold to collectors, a sad practice that has claimed many carousels over the last few decades. What fires, storms, and even recessions couldn't accomplish, a robust collectors' market did. Today the fiberglass Belle Freeman carousel has replaced the vintage attraction.

Although the 1955 fire destroyed more than fifty concessions, the town rallied, and the walkway was rebuilt for the opening of the next season. At the northern end of the boardwalk, Casino Pier was growing in strength and popularity. In response, Tunney organized a consortium of local businessmen from both Seaside Park and Seaside Heights to create Funtown U.S.A. (today Funtown Pier) on the border of the two towns. The new facility covered four full blocks from Dupont Avenue in Seaside Heights to Stockton Avenue in Seaside Park. By the spring of 1957, Funtown U.S.A. opened for business, offering eighteen major rides and fifteen kiddie rides. The Sky Ride, an elevated monorail, was their first major success. After that came the Sun Valley Bob, imported from Germany in 1961. In quick succession the consortium added rides with names like Roto Jet, Moon Shot, and Fly-O-Plane, and the crowds kept coming. The complex eventually featured more than 121 concessions, including skill games, food stands, and arcades. Another Funtown exclusive was the Wild Mouse, the first roller coaster on the boardwalk. Also popular was the Log Flume. Today the Tower of Fear is among the favorites, a ride that uses compressed air to send would-be daredevils more than 200 feet into the sky at high speed.

Fun in the Sun

Years after Freeman's Dentzel carousel established and anchored the southern end of the Seaside boardwalk, another carousel was installed on the walkway on what would become Casino Pier, predating other amusements there by five years. This machine had it roots in Burlington, New Jersey, where it operated at Island Beach Park until a fire swept through in 1928. The carousel was damaged but was rescued by a Princeton

Freeman's Amusements antique Illions carousel, which replaced the Dentzel carousel lost in the 1955 fire. This machine was dismantled and sold to collectors in the 1990s; it was replaced with a fiberglass machine. Pictured here riding the carousel a year before it was sold are Laurie and Jen Gabriel.

This carousel consists of beautifully hand-carved and painted figures from the golden age of the American carousel. Several master carousel carvers of the era are represented, including William Dentzel, Charles Looff, Charles Carmel, and Marcus Illions. Because the selection is not limited to horses but has camels, a lion, tiger, and a donkey, it is known as a "menagerie." It is called the Floyd L. Moreland Dentzel/Looff Carousel in honor of Dr. Floyd Moreland, who saved and restored the classic machine in the mid-1980s.

Above: Floyd L. Moreland Dentzel/Looff Carousel (details).

Right: Floyd L. Moreland Dentzel/Looff Carousel, 1910, including several figures carved in the 1890s.

resident, Linus Gilbert, who created what is known as a "mixed machine," a carousel that has figures created by more than one carver: William Dentzel (Gustav's son), Charles I. D. Looff, Charles Carmel, and Marcus Illions. He moved his machine to Seaside Heights in 1932 and placed it in a ten-sided, open-frame building. Unfortunately, the open enclosure exposed the fragile carousel to the elements, and neighbors often complained about the machine's band organ.

Five years after the carousel arrived on the boardwalk, the L. R. Gilbert Construction Company began adding amusements and concessions in the carousel building. What had been a sleepy fishing pier would soon develop into an amusement complex that challenged the well-established Freeman's Amusements in the southern sector on the Seaside Park–Seaside Heights border. Linus Gilbert surrounded his crown jewel, the carousel, with an expansive exhibition hall. Officially named the Seaside Heights Casino, the locals referred to it simply as the Casino. It grew exponentially over the next few decades. By 1963 the Casino had bragging rights to a 165-by-65-foot Olympic swimming pool that was advertised as the largest recirculating, chlorinated salt-water pool in the United States. The complex covered the beachfront block from Grant to Sherman Avenues and extended from the ocean with riparian rights to Boulevard. There was a roller rink and a monstrous ballroom that was a popular venue for summer dances. The amusement area provided a 500-foot ocean pier with thirty-five rides, along with dozens of games of chance and food and gift stands—even a popular nightclub.

To keep the crowds coming, Gilbert expanded seaward, adding new rides every season and establishing the origins of today's Casino Pier. In 1948 he sold the complex to a group of investors, and by the 1960s day-to-day management was taken over by Kenneth Wynne Jr., who expanded the pier and in 1962 added the Casino Pier's first roller coaster, the Wild Mouse. As did other successful promoters along the Jersey Shore, Wynne turned to European manufacturers to stay current with state-of-the-art attractions. A successful attorney and television producer, Wynne struck a deal with one European manufacturer to replace a ride each season with a newer version, thus always remaining one step ahead of the competition. An example of this unique agreement was the Himalaya ride that made its debut in 1963. Casino Pier was able to showcase six brand-new and improved

THE CAROUSEL

The carousel had its beginnings in Arabia, where skilled horsemen played a game in which a clay bottle filled with perfume was passed from rider to rider. The demanding game required expert riding and precise eye-hand coordination to transfer the container without breaking it. Once the bottle broke, the perfume was released, the game concluded, and the easily identified loser was teased by his comrades for the next few days.

Legend says that the Crusaders in the twelfth century brought the game home with them to Italy and France. The Italians called the game *carosello*, meaning "little war." The game evolved in Europe and next appeared at the court of Charles VIII of France. Called *carrousel* in French, it became a game of grand pageantry. In 1662 Le Grand Carrousel was played in the Parisian square still referred to as the Place du Carrousel.

One variation of carousel involved the medieval sport of ring piercing, in which skilled riders at breakneck speeds attempted to pierce a small ring with a lance. Primitive practice devices were created, with wooden horses attached to massive beams that rotated around a central pole. The largest (live) horses, or in some cases slaves, that could be found were used to provide the power to turn the "carousel" as privileged members of the court rode the wooden horses and honed their skills at ring piercing. It was only a matter of time before others in the court discovered that riding the new contraption was fun, and an industry was born.

Wood-carvers and craftsmen soon began building carousels, and their results started to show up at fairs and carnivals. Because genuine horse or human power was required to rotate the "roundabout," the size and weight of this new amusement game was limited. That would change in 1879, when Englishman Frederick Savage harnessed a steam engine to a roundabout. The device quickly evolved into the ride we know today. With weight no longer an issue, skilled wood-carvers began to create fanciful versions of everyday creatures, including horses, roosters, tigers, and even pigs, for their roundabouts. Only the wealthiest nobles could afford their own carousels, so wood-carvers devised a cheaper model, a single figure mounted on a set of rockers or wheels—the hobby horse.

There are reports of roundabouts operating in the United States as early as the 1820s, but it was not until Gustav A. Dentzel appeared on the American scene in 1867 that the roundabout, or carousel, industry began to prosper. The twenty-year-old immigrant from Germany established a cabinet shop in Philadelphia. His father, an itinerant carousel operator, had carved and assembled a roundabout that he would transport from village to village, where he earned a living at fairs and festivals. Gustav followed in his father's footsteps, eventually earning enough money to move to New York in 1867 and establish a carousel manufacturing business. He named the new enterprise G. A. Dentzel, Steam and Horsepower Caroussell [*sic*] Builder. Dentzel's machines were horse driven until the early 1880s, when Frederick Savage's steam-powered carousel made the new industry possible. The Industrial Revolution wed the hand carver's skill, and larger, more ornate carousels became a reality.

Carousels began appearing in what were known as "trolley parks," the forerunners of modern-day amusement parks. The first electric-powered trolley line was constructed in Richmond, Virginia, in 1888. Sites all over the country followed the Richmond lead and constructed electric trolley lines. Taking advantage of the fact that the electric companies charged a flat fee for the use of the power required to run the trolleys, they included in their master plan rail extensions to provide access to rural areas for future development. Many trolley firms searching for a way to maximize the return on their investment created simple amusement parks, or "trolley parks" as they were called, on inexpensive land at the end of the line. Thousands of people hopped onto the new means of transportation and filled the trolley parks on weekends and holidays. In many ways the development of trolley parks paralleled the development of boardwalks along the Jersey Shore. There were dance pavilions, picnic grounds, concession stands, games of chance, and, naturally, amusement rides. The Ferris wheel was introduced at the 1893 World's Columbian Exposition in Chicago, and these began appearing along with carousels at trolley parks.

Five years after the carousel was installed, the Casino Building was erected to house the carousel, arcade games, and concession stands. The next step for the owners of the fledging amusement center was to start building seaward by gradually expanding the boardwalk opposite the Casino Building. The well-established Freeman's Amusement pier can be seen in the distance.

Himalaya rides over the decade, from 1963 to 1973. In 1964 Wynne installed an exciting sky ride, a ski lift–style chair, which provided patrons with a bird's-eye view of his entire complex. The ride circled the pier, boardwalk, swimming pool, and roller rink.

That scourge of all wooden walkways, fire, paid a visit once again in June 1965. The final tally was over $2 million, as Casino Pier sustained significant damage, all caused by an errant spark from a welder's torch. It was only a shift in wind direction that prevented the entire complex from being reduced to ashes. The boardwalk property was too valuable not to move forward, and rebuilding began immediately. (As an example of the property's value, when the promoters sought to capitalize on the popularity of miniature golf, the answer to the

problem of space proved obvious and unusual—the rooftops of five concession stands.)

Wynne was a sophisticated businessman, but running an operation like Casino Pier also required the heart of a showman. In 1985 he discussed with a *New York Times* reporter how, in addition to spending hundreds of thousands of dollars on a trendy European ride, his job required "scheming how to re-theme the older rides." One of his legendary coups involved a common scrambler, a ride in which gondolas spin on several axes attached to a main axis that also turns. Wynne constructed a dome over the scrambler and installed disco lights and a $20,000 sound system. "Sitting outside under the sky it was just another ride that went around," he said, "Now it's the damndest sensation you ever felt. We went from

$30,000 to $200,000 in sales on it." By this time Wynne had acquired a partner, Bob Bennett, who would eventually take over the operation.

Seaside's busy north–south thoroughfare, Ocean Terrace, unfortunately ran into a section of the venerable Casino Building, and in the 1980s it was removed to provide the long-needed right-of-way. Today what appears to be a castle on the boardwalk is actually the surviving section of the Casino Building with a medieval facelift. The popular Sky Ride was razed as part of the redevelopment and replaced with a more sophisticated model. Instead of carrying the riders over the Casino Pier complex, the new version transports the passengers above the bustling boardwalk for a sixteen-block round-trip excursion. The 1980s also saw the end of the old saltwater pool complex, once the pride of the resort. It was razed to make room for Water Works, meeting the public's demand for water slides. It was an expensive gamble, but it paid off for the promoters.

The enterprise eventually passed from Wynne to Bennett, and in 2002 Bob Bennett surprised many Seaside loyalists by selling Casino Pier to the Storino clan, the owners of longtime competitor Jenkinson's Boardwalk, in Point Pleasant Beach. To the relief of Seaside "board rats," the new owners have continued to invest in Casino Pier, adding new attractions while reinventing some of the traditional favorites.

A highlight of the Casino Building, amid a variety of arcade games and concession stands, is the carousel. Originally called the Dentzel/Looff Carousel, after the two men who carved the majority of the figures, it has been renamed the Floyd L. Moreland Dentzel/Looff Carousel in honor of retired City University of New York classics professor Floyd L. Moreland. In the 1980s it was he who fought against breaking up the old carousel and selling the figures to collectors. Moreland had ridden the machine as a child and even operated it on summer breaks as a teenager and college student. The persistent professor eventually convinced the carousel's owner to allow him to restore the machine. Moreland spent that winter in the unheated Casino Building, and each season afterward, lovingly restoring everything from the carousel paintings to the incandescent lighting. Through his efforts the machine is as close to original as possible, including fifty-eight animals carved by William Dentzel and Charles Looff. Some are jumpers—horses that move up and down on a pole—and others are

The silver lining to the terrible conflagration of 1955 was Funtown USA, which like a phoenix, emerged from the ashes of the Freemen Amusements fire. This image from the early 1960s shows some of Funtown's earliest amusements. The miniature train was popular with young children. Fun Cups was an exciting elevated ride that circled the pier.

Games of chance and skill have always been an integral part of the boardwalk experience. The Seaside walkway is lined with them from Funtown Pier to Casino Pier.

The Funtown Pier's enclosed-cab Ferris wheel is one of the highest wheels in New Jersey.

standers—anchored to the platform. Most of the figures are horses, but because there are also camels, a lion, a tiger, and a donkey, the carousel is technically classified as a "menagerie."

The Boardwalk Today

Funtown Pier continues to anchor the southern end of the boardwalk, while Casino Pier remains a popular north-end attraction. The yellow-pine walkway in between the new major amusement centers is packed with food stands, souvenir shops, and skill games. Skee-Ball, a tradition on the Jersey Shore since the turn of the twentieth century and a Seaside institution, was invented in 1909 by J. D. Estes of Philadelphia. The popular game's original 36-foot-long alley made it impractical for most concession operators and difficult to play. By 1928 the alley was reduced to 14 feet, making it accessible to smaller locations. The shorter alley also gave children and the elderly a chance to compete.

Another Seaside tradition is Original Kohr's and Kohr's Frozen Custards. This boardwalk favorite traces its history to the Kohr brothers of York County, Pennsylvania. The family eventually parted ways based on a disagreement involving which Kohr brother invented the treas-

ured family recipe (still a family secret, but they do admit a key ingredient is whole eggs). One branch markets a version of the recipe in slick, sanitized, big corporate-style outlets. Another part of the clan professes that Elton D. Kohr, the youngest of the brothers, invented the recipe and brought his brothers into the family business. Elton established concessions in Asbury Park, Point Pleasant, Atlantic City, and Seaside Heights. Upon his death his legacy was divided and became Original Kohr's and Kohr's Frozen Custards, and these dedicated boardwalk merchants proudly serve the dessert from brightly colored Kohr's Frozen Custard stands that to Seaside and Point Pleasant "board rats" represent the Jersey Shore.

Although the amusements are updated regularly, and the town is forced to replace a full block of the yellow-pine boards each season, the Seaside walkway is a throwback to the 1950s, when boardwalks ruled the Jersey Shore. The mixed smells of sausage and pepper sandwiches, popcorn, and suntan oil create an aroma that could only mean boardwalk. Midway-style barkers challenging you to break a few balloons or spin a wheel to win a stuffed animal, the deafening sounds of the amusements, and the sound of the breakers at high tide are all part of the show.

Atlantic City

Saltwater taffy is an Atlantic City original. Legend has it that a confectioner's Boardwalk taffy stand was swamped by an unexpected storm. The next day, when a pretty young lady approached and asked for the sweet treat, the saddened merchant replied, "You mean saltwater taffy, don't you?" and an industry was born.

Atlantic City borrowed the idea of an Easter parade from New York City. First held in 1876, the parade soon became emblematic of Atlantic City. Millions attended the annual rite of spring dressed in the latest fashions no matter what the thermometer read.

On a bright, warm summer day in June 1918, the Atlantic City Boardwalk (the city adopted the word *Boardwalk* as a street name in 1896, thus a capital *B* is always used when referring to Atlantic City's walkway) was packed with families enjoying the warm sun on their face. Couples felt as if they were part of the Social Register as roller chairs transported them up and down. The Mystic Shriners had a parade scheduled and were dressed in their colorful, full regalia.

All at once a police officer noticed a lifeboat crammed with people on the ocean horizon. The alarm was raised, and everyone stopped what they were doing and ran to the surf to help. The lifeguards launched their boats, and the tourists, along with the fully dressed Shriners, went waist deep into the ocean to help guide the boat ashore. They helped twenty-nine cold and weary men, women, and children onto the beach and heard a bone-chilling tale. They were survivors of the steamship *Carolina* that had been torpedoed by a German U-boat almost two days earlier. They told how the submarine officer boarded their vessel and informed them he meant them no harm but was under orders to sink the ship. They were permitted to enter and launch the lifeboat, then watch from a distance as the *Carolina* was destroyed. In an endearing sign of the era, the *New York Times* reported that "the band of Lu Lu Temple of Philadelphia, which was parading down the Boardwalk from the Shriners' Hall, joined the crowd and as the boat swept in it struck up the 'Star-Spangled Banner.' The crowds cheered and many women wept."

Comedians Bud Abbott and Lou Costello with their wives, Betty Abbott and Ann Costello, on the great walkway in the 1940s.

The German U-boat commander watching this scene from a safe distance might have wondered where all these people came from, why some of them were dressed so oddly, if there was always a band, and what kind of wooden street was that along the beach. That's the story of Atlantic City.

First Wheel of Destiny

Like many of the regions that became Jersey Shore resorts, Absecon Island was a windswept, barren island, home to a handful of hardy members of the same family. It was originally known by the locals as Further Island, and it sure was. The Native Americans who fished and escaped the summer heat here called it *Absegami*, which roughly translates to "Little Sea Water." By the early nineteenth century, the island was occupied by the descendants of Revolutionary War veteran Jeremiah Leeds, who christened his new homestead Absecon Island.

Live shows were the entertainment trend in turn-of-the-twentieth-century Atlantic City; however, when the ever-resourceful John Lake Young installed the Flip-Flop Railroad on his Million Dollar Pier, it was an immediate success. He had the golden touch.

There would never have been an Atlantic City were it not for a country doctor with big dreams. Jonathan Pitney was a Columbia College–trained physician and a competent, dedicated medical man, but as he traveled from house to house on horseback, delivering babies and tending to the ill, he dreamed of becoming a "somebody." His early attempts in local politics were unsuccessful. Then one of his house calls took him to remote Absecon Island, and he became obsessed with a powerful idea. Medical men of the era believed that salt water and ocean air would cure just about anything, including insanity. Pitney thought, why not create a Cape May–type resort on the tiny island? The city to the south had been a favorite with the Philadelphia elite for decades, and most developers believed Cape May too well established to challenge them for the lucrative carriage trade. The county doctor believed otherwise. He felt that all he needed to challenge Cape May and create a Newport for Philadelphians was a railroad to carry them just 60 miles to his fantasy island.

Railroads were indeed changing the face of the country, as the ultimate high tech of the era. They were also very expensive, as Pitney quickly discovered when he unsuccessfully attempted to interest the public and state politicians in his "city by the sea." He and his "railroad to nowhere" were ridiculed. Not unlike today, money follows money, and Pitney knew he needed a powerful ally for his dream to ever become a reality. He found that person in thirty-year-old Samuel Richards, a member of a patrician family with vast land and industrial holdings in South Jersey and Philadelphia, and more importantly, a circle of equally wealthy friends and associates. Just as late-twentieth-century stockbrokers were inundated with calls from investors wishing to dip their toes in the Internet boom, men of means in the early nineteenth century wanted to become involved in the sexy technology of their era: railroads.

Records indicate that Richards and his powerful friends were less interested in Pitney's resort than they were in connecting their bog iron, glass, and other manufacturing interests with the major seaport and market of Philadelphia. But that didn't matter—in 1852 a charter was granted to the Camden and Atlantic Railroad, and Jonathan Pitney looked like he had finally grasped the gold ring on the carousel of destiny.

The model for the new Absecon Island resort followed the business model of other railroad-driven enterprises. Railroad officers gobbled up land on Absecon Island for pennies on the dollar from Leeds family members, who were happy to part with their barren seaside parcels. Not only would the land grow exponentially in value once the railroad was completed, a second bite of the apple would come when the new cottage and hotel owners began spending money on the only efficient way to travel and send freight to the resort—the Camden and Atlantic Railroad. The railroad's appetite was so voracious that the state legislature eventually passed a law prohibiting them from acquiring any additional land. But where there is a will, there is a way, and the railroad officers formed the Camden and Atlantic Land Company, which continued to buy up the small island. Before the new railroad reached Absecon Island, they owned more than 1,000 acres.

Left: An early-twentieth-century view of the Atlantic City Boardwalk and pavilions, just six years after the fifth, and final, Boardwalk was completed.

Above: An illustration published in *Harpers Weekly* of the windswept porch of the Hotel Brighton during a summer storm in 1889.

Below: Taken in 1911, this photo depicts the Atlantic City Boardwalk so crowded that the roller chair operators had difficulty gliding their patrons in and out of the traffic. The rolling chair was originally introduced as transportation for invalids. In a short time everyone wanted to be treated to a ride, and by 1905 "Why Don't You Try" (The Rolling Chair Song) became a favorite tune along the Boardwalk. Entrepreneur Harry Shill struck gold when he came up with the idea of turning the chairs into romantic two and three seaters. The chairs were outfitted with electric motors by the late 1940s.

Above: The Boardwalk provided an opportunity for members of the opposite sex to socialize in an era of rigid Victorian mores. Wearing pinback buttons bearing humorous phrases became a popular way to encourage conversation between strangers. There was even a "widow fad"—young women dressed in black, complete with veils, to attract attention from the thousands of young men congregating on the Boardwalk.

Right: Although boardwalk piers were not invented at Atlantic City, the resort certainly perfected them. This photograph, taken from the roof of the Chalfonte Hotel, shows the Steeplechase Pier, the famous Steel Pier, and the Garden Pier farther down the Boardwalk.

The railroad picked up an important asset in Philadelphia civil engineer Richard B. Osborne, who not only took over the reins of the railroad construction when the first engineer proved incompetent, but also had the vision to understand Pitney's dream and played an important role in designing the city. The goal was to carve out as many lots as possible, which meant clearing any natural feature that was in the way. More lots meant more profit. While suggested names for the new city included Ocean City, Strand, Bath, Surfing, and Sea-Beach, Osborne is credited with coming up with the winner. Legend has it that when he unrolled a large map of the new city at an investor meeting, printed across the

top in beautifully written, gold serif type were the words *Atlantic City*. His cityscape included expansive avenues that ran parallel to the sea, named after the world's great oceans and seas: Pacific, Atlantic, Arctic, Baltic, Mediterranean, and Adriatic. In a stroke of marketing genius, and with the dream that Atlantic City would become a national resort, the right-angle streets were named after states. The city was officially incorporated on March 3, 1854.

So, the first "wheel of destiny," the railroad wheel, came up a winner for the fledgling resort. Another wheel would have an entirely different effect less than a century later.

The first train from Philadelphia via Camden, New Jersey, with nine passenger cars, arrived at the uncompleted drawbridge on July 1, 1854. It was crammed with more than six hundred opinion makers, including newspaper writers, politicians, and investors. The passengers were ferried to the island and another train for the short ride to the railroad's hotel (by the next season a drawbridge eliminated the ferry transfer). Decades later proponents of the resort would wax poetic about the foresight of Pitney, Richards, and Osborne in choosing the location of America's Playground, some expressing a bizarre theory about the Gulf Stream inexplicably making a westward turn as it passed Atlantic City, providing the resort with tropical weather. Skeptics, and envious competitors, point out that Atlantic City was about where one would end up if you drew a straight line from the oceanless City of Brotherly Love to the Atlantic Ocean, and that accounted for its success. Philadelphia, with its legions of lower-middle-class and upper-lower-class semiprofessionals and laborers of the new industrialized economy, was bound to include a railroad-accessible seaside resort in its ever-expanding sphere, and Absecon Island fit the bill. Pitney's "railroad to nowhere" now had a destination.

The original promotional train ride was not without problems, for after being treated to a free meal at the partially completed massive United States Hotel, the opinion makers quickly became a free meal for the swarms of mosquitoes and notorious green-head flies that could bite right through heavy Victorian-era wool pants—it would take a quarter of a century for the resort to bring the fly and mosquito problem under control. Flesh wounds aside, the marketing scheme was a success, for when the train opened to the eager public on Independence Day three days later, it was booked solid for the 1854 season. These were not luxury trains. They had open cars and wooden planks for seats, and the burning engine spewed enough soot and ash that passengers were covered from head to toe by the time they arrived at the island. A linen duster was not a fashion statement, it was a necessity. Dust and grime aside, most

JOHN LAKE YOUNG: SHOWMAN, ENTREPRENEUR, AND CELEBRITY HOST

John Lake Young's Atlantic City success story began in 1891 when he and his financier pal, Stewart McShea, purchased the old Applegate's Pier, later renamed the Ocean Pier. Young showcased Sarah Bernhardt in her Atlantic City debut here.

Young dubbed himself with the rank of Captain—and it stuck. By the time Ocean Pier burned in 1912, Captain Young had already built his Million Dollar Pier. The massive pier contained a ballroom, hippodrome, exhibition hall, Greek temple, and the city's first aquarium. In the 1930s the Million Dollar Pier had a Seagram's sign installed on the roof that depicted an oval racetrack. Four electric horses ran the race around the sign every three minutes, the winner alternating each time. Many a bet was placed on which horse would come in first.

Captain Young knew the value of free publicity and made it easy on the press by building his own home at the end of his Million Dollar Pier—the address, Number One, Atlantic Ocean. The villa, appointed with furniture commissioned in Europe, was featured in major newspapers. The home and its formal gardens were outlined with thousands of tiny electric bulbs, a display designed by Young's fishing buddy and frequent houseguest, Thomas Edison. Young entertained most of the celebrities of the era, including President Taft.

Young and McShea's Pier.

Young's Million Dollar Pier, built in 1906.

Young's Italian villa home at Number One, Atlantic Ocean.

President William Taft dining at Young's villa on the Million Dollar Pier.

The lobby of the Traymore Hotel, designed by William L.
Price in 1915, announced to its guests that they "had arrived."

of the passengers disembarking on the island were happy to escape the sweltering city.

The permanent population of Atlantic City grew slowly, adding only about five hundred residents from 1855 to 1865. Several hotels and boardinghouses joined the United States Hotel in welcoming guests, and the original land speculators increased their wealth. Few amenities existed, and even the bathhouses were crudely constructed and dragged to higher ground at the end of the season. The Civil War no doubt played a part in the resort's sluggish growth, but historians differ on what may have been the real issue. Cape May also proved a tough competitor for the wealthy Philadelphia patrons. In addition, the railroad experienced numerous growing pains, including bad weather and the lack of capital to improve the line, and came close to going bankrupt in the nationwide financial panic of 1857. But by the early 1870s the railroad was paying a dividend, carrying more passengers—almost a half million in 1874—and it appeared that the development plan was back on track.

Jonathan Pitney achieved the financial success and prestige he always dreamed of, and died in 1869 in Absecon Village. However, his younger and more aggressive partner, Samuel Richards, believed that Atlantic City had much further to go. He realized that in order to tap the demographic group that would flood the Boardwalk, excursion houses, and boardinghouses, the Camden and Atlantic Railroad would need to lower its fares. Records indicate that the railroad was charging $3.00 for a round-trip ticket, $2.00 for a one-way fare.

The Steel Pier as seen from the beach.

Aerial view of the Steel Pier.

THE STEEL PIER

The most successful and well-known pier in Atlantic City was the Steel Pier. Built in 1898 opposite Virginia Avenue, it opened with a guest appearance by Annie Oakley. The pier extended 1,600 feet over the Atlantic and featured a casino, theater, dance pavilion, and an aquarium with sea lions. Over 3,500 electric lights outlined the magnificent structure.

One of the secrets of the pier's success was its "all attractions for the price of one" admission policy. Known as the "Showplace of the Nation," the sign said it all: RUDY VALLEE IN PERSON, BIG CIRCUS, DANCING, DIVING HORSES. The latter was a tremendous draw—to the amazement of the crowds, horse and rider would plunge 45 feet into an 11-foot-deep tank.

Entertainment giants from Frank Sinatra to the Rolling Stones have also performed at the Steel Pier. But even the most successful promoters can have a bad day: George Hamid, who ran the pier for three decades, had one when he turned down an appearance by a young Elvis Presley. Hamid said later that he thought no one would pay to see someone with such an odd name.

Entrance to the Steel Pier.

The famous High Diving Horse.

Richard tried in vain to convince his fellow officers, but they would not budge.

Not to be denied, Richards and two other officers joined with nine other investors to create the new "no frills" Philadelphia and Atlantic Railroad in 1877, breaking ground on April 1. To keep costs down, they chose to construct a narrow-gauge railroad with a 3½-foot track gauge instead of the standard 4 feet, 8½ inches of other railroads. The Camden and Atlantic Railroad invested $40,000 a mile to build their standard railroad, while the narrow gauge came in at less than $13,000 a mile. The smaller gauge was also less labor intensive to construct, and the entire project was completed in a record-breaking ninety days. The Philadelphia and Atlantic Railroad lowered prices to $1.25 for a round-trip ticket, $1.00 for one-way fares. The railroad even ran special excursion day trips with round-trip fares of only 50 cents. True, the company's officers had big dreams but little money, and built their station from bits and pieces of buildings from Philadelphia's 1876 Centennial Exposition. But Richards was correct. Although the railroad itself did not make money, the genie was out of the bottle. The Philadelphia and Atlantic Railroad broke the back of the one-line monopoly, resulting in permanent competitive pricing. The gates to Atlantic City were opened to the lower-middle-class and upper-lower-class families who would account for its ultimate success.

The narrow-gauge line was eventually taken over by the Pennsylvania Railroad and converted to a standard-gauge track line that provided plusher and more comfortable passenger cars. Train travel in general had improved since the first wood-burning engine left Camden for Absecon Island in 1854, and the trip could now be made in an hour and a half. It was now possible to spend Sunday at the beach and be back at the office, store counter, or factory on Monday morning. Contrary to popular belief, the lower-tier white- and blue-collar workers who took advantage of this faster, less expensive means of travel did spend money in the resort. With the exception of the dreaded "shoobies"—cheapskates who would travel on a 50-cent round-trip Excursion Special with their lunch stored under their seat in an old shoe box—the new class of traveler ate in the restaurants and left behind hard-earned nickels and dimes before boarding the evening train back to Philadelphia. Many would save for a year and take a one-week vacation at the resort, staying at one of the more reasonable hotels or boardinghouses.

Above: Another icon of the Atlantic City Boardwalk is the Miss America Pageant. The big show began in 1921 as an intercity beauty contest sponsored by the local newspapers. Public criticism closed the pageant in 1928, but after a few false starts it became a permanent attraction in 1935. Norman Rockwell was one of the first judges in the early 1920s.

Below: In 1952 Marilyn Monroe, visiting Atlantic City to promote a new film, filled in as the Miss America parade's grand marshal. However, her "revealing" outfit was at odds with the wholesome appearance expected of pageant contestants, and she was not invited back.

The Boardwalk today.

The Amusement Pier as it now looks.

Boardwalk with a Capital *B*

As noted in the prologue, Atlantic City, a city of firsts, has laid claim to creating the first boardwalk on the Jersey Shore. While this honor in truth belongs to Cape May's "flirtation walk," Atlantic City does own the title of putting the capital *B* in *Boardwalk*, and building the biggest, busiest, and brightest wooden walkway in the world.

The original Atlantic City Boardwalk was not created to shake the change from the pockets of the tourists, but rather to simply keep the sand out of the hotels and the now-plush passenger train cars. Two local businessmen, Jacob Keim and Alexander Boardman, sold the idea of a portable wooden walkway, just 18 inches above the sand, to a fledgling resort tired of sweeping sand out of the hotels and trains. On May 9, 1870, the city voted on their idea and passed a resolution to construct a new "board walk." Several forward-thinking hotel owners feared that concession stands on this new walkway would block their ocean view, and the city agreed to pass an ordinance prohibiting building within 30 feet of the boardwalk. This would not last long.

Once the $5,000 was raised, the walkway was constructed, and on June 26, 1870, a Boardwalk parade, soon to be an Atlantic City tradition, was held. Philadelphian Gustav Dentzel, the master carver and carousel maker, was probably one of this boardwalk's first amusement operators. His father had made a good living in Germany as a carousel carver and itinerant dream maker as he would cart his colorful musical machine from village to village. Likewise, Gustav transported a carousel on the Camden and Atlantic Railroad and erected it in the vicinity of the railroad excursion house. He became wealthy enough from his carousel in Atlantic City to establish himself as one of the most prolific carousel firms in the country, famous throughout the United States.

After the second and eventually third railroads were added, the Boardwalk was unable to cater to the massive summer crowds, and a series of new walkways were constructed. Another portable Boardwalk was built in the spring of 1880, 14 feet wide, at the identical level as the first. During this period entrepreneurs began to realize that there was money to be made on this wood-planked beach road. From its creation money greased the political machine wheels in Atlantic City, and in a short time the merchants convinced the city government to allow building within 10 feet of the Boardwalk. (Bathhouses still had to be at least 15 feet away.) According to *Butler's Book of the Boardwalk*, published in 1952, "Owners of the buildings had them set up on pilings higher than the Boardwalk to allow the tides to flow beneath them, and each structure was connected to the 'Walk by a ramp."

Samuel Richards's theory about lower-cost transportation opening the city to a new class of people was right on the money. By 1883 the hoards of day-trippers could avail themselves to more than a hundred permanent businesses along the Boardwalk, with another hundred transient seasonal kiosks and fifty-two bathhouses lining the oceanfront. The 1883 Atlantic City directory also listed four small hotels, four guest cottages, two piers, fifteen restaurants, and numerous stores.

Piers became an interesting phenomenon along the Boardwalk, and although the resort did not invent the ocean pier, it would eventually become emblematic of Atlantic City. The first pier was built by the resort's third railroad, the West Jersey and Atlantic Railroad, to com-

plement its Excursion House. (The West Jersey and Atlantic Railroad would eventually merge with the Camden and Atlantic to form the West Jersey and Seashore Line.)

The pier opened on the same day the first West Jersey and Atlantic train arrived in town to much excitement. There were free meals for the newspaper reporters and politicians, enough speeches to fill a hot-air balloon, and a brass band to keep everyone awake. The concept was simple: Provide a location for picnics, concerts, and other amusements across from your station and hold on to your customers. At any given time a selection of snake charmers, portable merry-go-rounds, minstrel shows, and even a "learned pig" could be found to provide entertainment for the trainloads of people seeking a break from their humdrum six-days-a-week work schedule. The pier was made of wood, about 500 feet long, and was destroyed by a storm that same year.

The Blenheim Hotel, 1906. Constructed of concrete, the Blenheim was designed by Philadelphia architect William L. Price, a pioneer in the use of reinforced concrete for large-scale buildings. The materials were purchased from Thomas Edison's Portland Cement Company, and Edison helped supervise the construction.

The Iron Pier, which opened in 1886, was too far from the busy commercial sector to turn a profit. The H. J. Heinz Company bought it in 1898 and extended it a thousand feet over the ocean. The company gave free pickles and pins to visitors until the pier was destroyed by the Great Atlantic Hurricane of 1944. The famous 57 Varieties sign can be seen on the building at the end of the pier.

The next promoter to attempt a pier was Colonel George W. Howard from Baltimore. His pier was opened on July 12, 1882, with an expansive entertainment pavilion at the end of the fragile 650-foot wooden structure. Howard offered amusements ranging from vaudeville to concerts, but the Atlantic Ocean—unhappy with this encroachment over its domain—claimed the enterprise in a nasty storm just two months after opening day.

While new piers were in the planning stage, the Boardwalk had been illuminated with a series of open-arc electric lights in 1882, located where each street met the walkway. Merchants also added lights, turned on from May to the end of August. During this same time, driving carriages on the beach was popular, so a system of ramps was installed to allow horse and carriage to cross the busy walkway.

By the summer of 1884 another Boardwalk was required to keep up with the trainloads of revelers arriving daily. This time a 20-foot-wide wooden walkway was installed 5 feet off the sand, and it extended 2 miles, from Rhode Island Avenue to Iowa Avenue. Although the city saw no need for a railing, there were frequent reports of young men and women falling off. The cause, the *Atlantic Review* reported on Saturday, August 15, 1885, was, "in nearly every instance, the parties [were] flirting." It was not unusual to read of reports of broken bones.

In 1883, a year before the new boardwalk opened, the tenacious Colonel Howard built another pier. This time he included three pavilions and extended the wooden midway 600 feet over the ocean. That winter a storm drove a schooner into the ill-fated pier, severing the two outer pavilions. But Mother Howard didn't raise any quitters, and the colonel rebuilt his pier the following season. It stood until the city claimed it under the eminent domain rule in 1889.

The next attempt at a pier was undertaken by James R. Applegate, owner of a popular photography studio at Tennessee Avenue. His double-decker, 626-foot pier, opposite his studio, opened on June 1, 1884. Applegate's Pier boasted space for more than 10,000 people and was known for its public ice-water fountain that during the dog days of summer used 3,000 pounds of ice daily. The pavilion also had facilities for dances, band concerts, contests, and picnics.

The race was on. Whoever could construct a longer pier, and keep King Neptune from taking it for a sail, could accommodate the largest crowds and have boardwalk bragging rights. After Applegate's Pier came the city's first pier constructed on iron pilings, opening on April 25, 1886. Although the owners provided first-class entertainment, its location at the foot of Massachusetts Avenue, in what was becoming the residential section of the Boardwalk, doomed it to failure from the start. Location, location, location was as important then as now. They sold the pier to the H. J. Heinz Company in 1898. The Heinz Ocean Pier, although enlarged and extended 1,000 feet into the Atlantic, was never a commercial success—even though it was open all year long and everyone left with a souvenir pickle pin and delicious free sample. Then the Great Atlantic Hurricane of 1944 cut the "Pickle Pier" in two, and hurled 50-foot sections of it across the Boardwalk and into the memory books.

Before the next noteworthy pier was created, the city would enlarge and improve the Boardwalk on two more occasions. The 24-foot-wide fourth Boardwalk (built in large part because of the damage the 1889 hurricane did to the third Boardwalk) opened for business on May 10, 1890, with fireworks and a festive parade. Because the previous Boardwalk was covered in up to 6 feet of water during a hurricane, it was decided to raise the new walk to a height of 10 feet from the sand, complete with substantial railings on both sides. The new Boardwalk extended from Caspian Way to Albany Avenue.

The Golden Era

The fifth and final Boardwalk was built six years later in 1896, the same year a city ordinance adopted "Boardwalk" as a street and the official spelling of the word. The new, 40-foot-wide promenade now rested on powerful steel pilings and girders, constructed by the Phoenix Bridge Company. Before this substantial investment, the city took care of some important business. The Beach Park Act, passed by the New Jersey State legislature in 1894, essentially granted Atlantic City the right of eminent domain over its extremely valuable beachfront. The city passed its own ordinance in 1899, drew up easement deeds with the property owners, and subsequently controlled a 60-foot right-of-way along the beachfront. Land owners along the Boardwalk were granted permission by Atlantic City to build as many piers as their wallets would permit—as long as they were a minimum of 1,000 feet long and had only one entrance.

On July 8, 1896, the Boardwalk parade and dedication took place in grand style, including the mayor's wife driving the final "golden" spike into the last plank to mark the beginning of the celebration. It was promptly stolen and never seen again. The joke was on the thief, however, for it was an ordinary iron spike with gold paint. But the golden era of the Atlantic City Boardwalk had arrived.

The Easter parade in Atlantic City drew unprecedented crowds.

The Breakers hotel debuted as the Hotel Rudolf around 1909. In the 1920s, it was enlarged, modernized, and renamed The Breakers. This elegant hotel catered to Atlantic City's Jewish patrons, strictly observing kosher laws.

No longer just a series of wooden planks used to keep the sand out of hotels and trains, the Boardwalk had become a destination. It wasn't the city, and it wasn't the beachfront, it was a magical promenade. If Atlantic City was a land of illusions, then the Boardwalk was the Yellow Brick Road, and once you experienced it, you damn well knew you weren't in Kansas anymore.

The clerks, secretaries, teachers, salespeople, and factory workers who contributed the money that drove the Atlantic City machine could take the train from Philadelphia for just $1.00, change in an excursion house into their best ready-made suit or dress, and promenade along the walkway in an anonymous throng

of humanity. Walking next to you could be the likes of "Diamond Jim Brady" or his longtime girlfriend, the actress Lillian Russell. What a story to tell the crowd back at the mill or the office!

At a time when a woman would not be seated for dinner alone at a plush hotel, and when computer dating was a century away, young men and women could make social contact with strangers, a rare occurrence during the Victorian era. This is what made promoter George Tilyou so successful. His Steeplechase Pier, which opened in 1902, when he purchased the unsuccessful Auditorium Pier in Atlantic City, was patterned after his popular Steeplechase Park in Coney Island. Tilyou's rides and attractions always had the goal of mixing the sexes in an undignified, exciting, and daring pile of humanity, whether on his Human Roulette Wheel or the Giant Slide.

Boardwalk Icons

Rolling chairs were not an Atlantic City original, but adopted from the 1876 Centennial Exposition. Hardware store owner William Hayday introduced them to the city as a way for the handicapped to see the Boardwalk. The chairs experienced modest success until another entrepreneur, Harry Shill, came up with the idea of making two- and three-seater models. His adaptation was a hit, and soon the wicker rolling chairs were the rage of the walkway, becoming synonymous with the expansive Boardwalk. Rolling chairs had a dual purpose. On one level they provided practical basic transportation on the long Atlantic City Boardwalk. But they also gave clerks and factory workers the opportunity to be served, to enter a world foreign to them if only for ten minutes. You might be rolling along the great walkway next to the owner of your factory.

Another Boardwalk icon was saltwater taffy. Legend has it that a confectioner named David Bradley had his uncovered taffy stand swamped by an unexpected storm. The next day, when a pretty, young girl approached and asked for the sweet treat, the saddened merchant replied, "You mean saltwater taffy, don't you?," and an industry was born. Another version has Bradley making French toffee in the evening and leaving his open cart exposed to the nightly sea breeze to permit the confection to cool. Both stories are no doubt pure Atlantic City hype, as there is definitely no salt water in saltwater taffy. Anyone who has sat too close to the incoming surf

A different kind of animal—literally—in the hotel business was Lucy, the elephant. The ninety ton, 65-foot-high pachyderm began life as an attraction to promote real estate sales. A distant cousin of the Light of Asia in Cape May and the Elephant Hotel (or Elephantine Colossus) in Coney Island, she is the only surviving relative. Lucy has done her stint as a hotel, tavern, and even a summer cottage. She was going to ruins when a group of preservationists saved her and moved her to nearby Margate. Lucy is now a National Historic Landmark.

and had an article of food come in contact with ocean water can attest that salt water and food do not mix. The real innovation came when Joseph Fralinger, using the gimmicky name of saltwater taffy, came up with the concept of selling his candy in takeout boxes. The brightly colored containers made a wonderful souvenir to carry or mail home, and in a short time Fralinger's motto, "Famous the World Over," was a reality. He became a genuine Atlantic City success story.

The Steel Pier

In 1898 the Steel Pier, the most successful pier in the resort's long history, opened with an appearance by famed sharpshooter Annie Oakley. It was located opposite Virginia Avenue and the bathhouses owned by George W. Jackson, the president of the newly formed Atlantic City Steel Pier Company. In an effort to engineer a stable structure that would be impervious to the nasty Atlantic storms, massive iron pilings were driven into the sand, and a steel skeleton extended 1,600 feet from the Boardwalk, its sturdy frame topped with a hardy wooden deck. Next came the buildings that lined the pier, dazzling both tourists and permanent residents alike. The stylish Casino Building, with two stately towers, served as the entrance to the pier. To squeeze the most space out of the available square footage, it was a double-decker. The first level was a large esplanade, perfect for people-watching and catching a refreshing sea breeze. The floor above served as the Casino Theatre, host to many of the great bands of the day. Next built was the almost 12,000-square-foot dance pavilion, behind which was a monstrous aquarium where people gathered to watch the sea lions. In Atlantic City nothing succeeded like excess, and the icing on the cake was the almost 3,500 electric lights outlining the structures. The Steel Pier was a wondrous site to behold, and it drew people to it like moths to a candle.

Instead of a "pay as you play" model, the owners of the new pier created a marketing plan that permitted entrance to the pier and all it had to offer for one flat price, a dime. From opening day the Steel Pier was a smash hit, providing band music, dances, and water shows, and even introducing the latest dance craze, the

cakewalk, to the country. No trip to Atlantic City was complete without a visit. During the first half of the twentieth century, everybody who was anybody, or wanted to be somebody, appeared here, at the "Showplace of the Nation." Bud Abbott and Lou Costello, Frank Sinatra, Glenn Miller, Jackie Gleason, Benny Goodman, Bob Hope, Amos 'n' Andy, and even the Three Stooges played the pier. In the 1960s such acts as the Rolling Stones and the Beach Boys followed a generation of stars to the Steel Pier. The pier even hosted the Miss America Pageant for a short time in the 1930s. Two of the pier's memory makers were the Diving Bell, in which up to fifteen riders took a trip below the waves, and, of course, the High Diving Horse, an act in which a rider and horse jumped from an elevated platform 45 feet into an 11-foot-deep tank. Other attractions ranged from legitimate entertainment to curiosities like Alvin "Ship-wreck" Kelly, who set a record in 1930 when he sat atop a flagpole on a 13-inch disk for forty-nine days. His record was not broken for over thirty years. If the public would pay to see it, the pier would provide it. From the human cannonball to boxing cats, the Steel Pier had it all.

Above: Everything at Atlantic City was larger than life, including this giant Underwood typewriter. It was exhibited in the Garden Pier's "Products and Progress" pavilion for almost two decades, before being relocated to Convention Hall. The machine was fully operational and actually printed via a remote-control device. It was scrapped for the war effort during World War II.

Young's Million Dollar Pier

A genuine Atlantic City character who would leave his mark on the resort's amusement industry, John Lake Young was originally hired by carousel maker Gustav Dentzel as a manager for his amusement business. Young assisted the German immigrant with language problems, and he was also quite handy around the carousels. After watching Dentzel become wealthy collecting all of those pennies and nickels spinning his beautiful, hand-carved carousel, the energetic Young tried his hand at various Boardwalk businesses himself. What he lacked in capital he more than made up in energy and personality.

After his stint with Dentzel and other ventures, Young became an Atlantic City policeman. While patrolling the Boardwalk, he experienced one of those serendipitous meetings that change an individual's life forever. He met and befriended retired wealthy businessman Stewart McShea, and the two men discussed various schemes to cash in on the Boardwalk boom. From his

Right: The Garden Pier, once host to the likes of John Philip Sousa, Harry Houdini, and Rudy Valee, was distinguished by beautiful gazebos, shrubbery, and even a pond. Today its sturdy skeleton supports the Atlantic City Arts Center and the city museum.

days with Dentzel, Young had an affinity for carousels, and he was familiar with the amount of money his former employer had made. McShea provided the capital, they formed a partnership, and together they purchased a brand-new, beautifully carved machine. The aggressive Young wanted to operate the carousel seven days a week, but his partner, a devote Christian, did not want the machine to run on the Sabbath. Their compromise: The carousel organ played spiritual songs on Sundays, while the carousel took the day off.

The duo's next step was to acquire the less than successful Applegate's Pier in 1891, renaming it Young and McShea's Pier. With the latter's capital and the former's energy and Barnum-like showmanship, the new venture was a success. Nineteenth-century diva Sarah Bernhardt made her Atlantic City debut at the new pier. Young, always with an eye for a new attraction, also installed the Flip-Flop Railroad, a primitive thrill ride, on his pier. He had the golden touch.

Somewhere along the way the showman appointed himself a captain, and the name stuck. With the fortune he was amassing, and spending around town, the name was fine with his cronies, especially when he announced Young's Million Dollar Pier, which opened at the end of Arkansas Avenue on June 26, 1906. As described by historian William McMahon in *So Young . . . So Gay! The Story of the Boardwalk, 1870–1970*, it was "a glittering palace with the world's largest ballroom, a hippodrome, exhibit hall, Greek temple, the city's first aquariums and deep sea net hauls." The last item was something Young began at his original pier: Crowds would gather around a trapdoor until, at a given signal, a crew of men opened the door and pulled in a net full of fish, shellfish, and some sea creatures that many believe were not even native to the mid-Atlantic shoreline. No matter; the crowds loved it, and their patronage helped the showman finance his next attraction.

Young knew the value of getting his name in the newspapers. The Captain built a stunning Italianate villa at the end of his Million Dollar Pier and assigned himself the address Number One, Atlantic Ocean. He loved electric lights almost as much as he loved publicity, and with some expert assistance from his good friend Thomas

The Chalfonte Hotel, the first fireproof hotel erected in Atlantic City, opened on July 2, 1904. Its palatial Renaissance style appealed to America's wealthy "captains of industry," who thought of themselves as heirs of the "merchant princes" of fifteenth-century Italy.

The legendary Blenheim Hotel catered to the East Coast's industrial elite. The luxury hotel was later razed to make room for Bally's Park Place, a gaming casino and hotel.

Edison, his villa was strung from the foundation to the top of its dome with thousands of tiny lights. Other guests to Number One, Atlantic Ocean included the incomparable Harry Houdini, candidate Teddy Roosevelt, and President William H. Taft. Captain John Lake Young was a positive role model in Atlantic City, where he earned his fortune honestly, unlike many politicians, bootleggers, gamblers, and brothel owners who provided a different type of entertainment in "America's Playground."

Second Wheel of Destiny

For most of the first half of the twentieth century, Atlantic City maintained its dominance as the Jersey Shore's most popular travel location and a resort with a positive national reputation. Its massive Convention Hall had a major share of its namesake lucrative business. Built without pillars, the building claimed the world's largest unobstructed view when it was completed in 1929.

Although Atlantic City was never a serious rival of Newport, Rhode Island, or Saratoga Springs, New York, for those who could afford them it offered a string of luxury hotels, such as the Marlborough-Blenheim and the Traymore. For most of the strollers on the great wooden walkway they were just places to stop, dream a bit, and perhaps have your photograph taken.

World War II marked the beginning of a downward spiral from which the old resort never recovered. Blackouts and dim-outs along the Boardwalk, shortages of material, and, more importantly, a lack of tourists threw some of the hotels in the red for the first time, and many had no idea how to react. In the short term the hotels covered their expenses courtesy of Uncle Sam. From 1942 to 1946 Atlantic City Camp Boardwalk came into existence, as hundreds of thousands of armed service personnel trained in Convention Hall and bivouacked in many of the luxury Boardwalk hotels. Some of the hotels were also converted to convalescent facilities.

Sadly, after the war, cracks began to appear in the veneer of the once-great resort. Many families stopped vacationing in Atlantic City, while the soldiers were enjoying some of the seedier attractions—ones that had always been available, but were separated from the family "fun in the sun" illusion. To make matters worse, this loss of the regular tourist trade revenue prevented many of the hotels and amusement piers from modernizing or even maintaining their facilities.

The transportation monopoly that Atlantic City owned for a century was quickly disappearing, and the second wheel of destiny that came into play in the latter part of the twentieth century was not kind to America's Playground. That wheel belonged to the automobile. And while the country may have been wild about the

Atlantic City–inspired game, Monopoly, they began looking for other places to spend their vacation.

Once the war ended and the ex-soldiers began to enjoy one of the most robust postwar economies in history, they discovered that their automobiles gave them a freedom the railroads could never equal. Atlantic City historians tell how back in the day one of the grand hotels, the Brighton, would not permit guests who arrived in a horseless carriage to check into the facility. Supposedly the noise annoyed one of the owners. Perhaps it was so, but I like to think the Brighton owner knew the automobile would eventually do in his bustling city by the sea.

Atlantic City could not survive and prosper without the loyalty of the generations of families who had vacationed there—whether a wealthy family with steamer trunks who stayed at the resort for the summer, or any of the millions of blue-collar workers who took the same train, even if just for a day or a weekend, frequenting the same piers and restaurants year after year. After World War II,

many of these people threw their rigid train schedule away and took their automobile just about anywhere they pleased. If they traveled to Atlantic City, it might just be for a few hours on the beach. Dine on your picnic lunch, change in the car, and, maybe, buy a box of saltwater taffy. To exacerbate things, Atlantic City was not designed for cars, so many people chose resorts like Wildwood, where motels with parking lots seemed to be everywhere.

Another nail in the coffin of the once great city came in the form of safe and reliable air travel. Why gamble on the weather on the Jersey Shore when you could fly the family to Florida, or islands south, for your fun in the sun? As the railroads lost business, they consolidated and eventually curtailed and virtually eliminated passenger service.

In an effort to hold on to whatever business they could, the city permitted motels to be built on the outskirts of town. As a result, fewer tourists frequented the city cen-

The convention industry represented a major asset to the resort. The Atlantic City Auditorium, known as Convention Hall, was dedicated on May 31, 1929.

ter, and many of the regulars, finding that the facilities and service had deteriorated, left and never returned. Atlantic City's dirty little secret, that the emperor was naked, came to the nation's attention when the Democratic Party held its convention there in 1964. The candidate, Lyndon Johnson, was a shoe-in, so the national reporters turned their cameras on the city, finding hotels anything but first class, piers suffering from a lack of maintenance, and poverty everywhere. The country didn't like what it saw on the little screen, and fewer and fewer people had any interest in the city that had played host to millions over the past century. Hotel owners began bailing out, selling their aging grand ladies to investors who quickly realized they had been taken for a ride, Atlantic City style, when they wondered where all the tourists went. As the grand hotels began disappearing, one historian compared the view of the Boardwalk to a beautiful woman missing a few teeth. Mayors went to prison as the political machine that managed for over a century to juggle organized crime,

motherhood, and apple pie without dropping a ball finally broke down. The last deadly blow was the "white flight" that took place in record numbers, as wealthier white residents left the city, deserting their black neighbors, who, along with their great-grandparents, had played a major role in the success of America's Playground.

Third Wheel of Destiny

The city appeared doomed and drifted into a long, dreary sleep with an occasional glimpse of life, like the national publicity of the Miss America Pageant. But even that soured as angry feminists marched on the old Boardwalk. An attempt to resurrect the old High Diving Horse attraction was stopped midair by animal rights activists. It seemed that Atlantic City was in the wrong place at the wrong time. A popular bumper sticker in those days read, "The last one out, turn out the lights."

The interior of Convention Hall was in 1929 the largest space constructed without pillars or roof posts.

The new Atlantic City Convention Center opened in 1997.

Boardwalk Hall, which first opened as Convention Hall in 1929, was recently restored to host a variety of special events, including the Miss America pageant.

Just as the town seemed about to become an old memory, the permanent domain of the poor and elderly, another wheel of fate came into play—the roulette wheel, along with its other gaming pals. If casino gambling had turned a Nevada desert town into a golden oasis, perhaps it could breathe new life into an ailing city by the sea. It wasn't an easy task. Antigambling sentiments ran deep in the religious community, and the supporters' initial attempt to pass a referendum legalizing casino gambling in New Jersey in 1974 failed. Pastors weekly reminded their congregations about the evils of gambling, and the wording of the referendum didn't help. If passed, it would have made gambling legal in the entire state at the option of the various municipalities. The second attempt, in 1976, was a success, with the referendum approved by over 350,000 voters. With financial campaign assistance from potential private casino operators (casino gambling would not be run as a state bureaucracy, which people feared in the 1974 proposal), a promise to use a portion of the revenues to lower New Jersey's steep property taxes and to support senior citizens and the handicapped, along with limiting of casino gambling to Atlantic City, it proved an easy victory. Resorts International opened for business in 1978 to record crowds.

Atlantic City had rolled the dice and once again became one of the country's most popular travel destinations. More than a dozen casinos and ancillary businesses have created more than 100,000 jobs in the region, and the Garden State Parkway is the new road to riches. Parades of cars, limos, and tour buses arrive, packed with men and women hoping to hit it big—or just have fun trying. The bright, brassy, expensive casinos operate twenty-four/seven, and most visitors will admit that they do not travel to Atlantic City for the Boardwalk or the ocean. It is estimated that while nongaming revenues in the famous Las Vegas "Strip" are above 50 percent, the number is a paltry 20 percent in Atlantic City. Many of the hotel/casinos ironically chose to offer no window views of their major asset, the Atlantic Ocean, in an attempt to focus people on the business at hand: gaming. Some experts feel that, instead of rebuilding the aging resort, legalized gaming has spurred suburban growth similar to Las Vegas. Although the Casino Control Act envisioned legalized gaming as a unique tool for urban redevelopment, the legislators mandated that all gaming take place in the confines of the casinos. The act did this "to assure that the existing nature and tone of the hospitality industry in New Jersey and Atlantic City is preserved . . . and that casino rooms . . . are always offered and maintained as an integral element of such hospitality facilities, rather than as the industry unto themselves that they become in other jurisdictions." Instead of revitalizing the city as promised, the casinos have, for the most part, become self-contained islands similar in profile to their cousin out west.

Sand sculptors, popular along the Boardwalk, profited from admiring tourists who tossed coins onto blankets by their art-work. The city eventually stopped the practice after discovering that some of the sculptors added mortar to the sand to prevent the waves from reclaiming their creations.

Back to the Future

Today the city's piers are just a memory, with the exception of the Steel Pier, which has been turned into an amusement pier, and the Garden Pier, home to the Atlantic City Art Center and the city museum. Most of the old hotels have fallen prey to the wrecker's ball and new development. But starting in 1985, the casino businesses were required to contribute 1.25 percent of their gross revenues to the Casino Reinvestment Development Authority (CRDA). That's a good deal of money earmarked to rebuild the city and assist with new casino development. Curtis Bashaw, the executive director of CRDA, believes that "at the CRDA we want to let the past inform the future." He feels that a resort with 150 years of history that once possessed "one of the most storied skylines of the early 20th century, with an attraction in the Boardwalk that was known around the world," should allow these roots to guide future development. Bashaw's back-to-the-future philosophy is no doubt based on his experience in Cape May, a resort that became a storybook success and a National Historic Landmark by preserving and respecting its past.

There is no argument that without legalized gaming in New Jersey, America's Playground would have slipped into oblivion. There are even reports that beach use is increasing, and, as always, the oceanfront at Atlantic City is still free. The old resort has the required DNA to once again establish itself. Jonathan Pitney's "railroad to nowhere" created a unique resort, a living experiment in tourism that has been on a roller-coaster ride for over a century and a half—and things are just starting to get exciting.

Ocean City

Boardwalk piers were always the rage. The promoter purchased the rights to the boardwalk entrance and built his wooden dynasty as far out to sea as his wallet and nature allowed. Most piers were outlined with small electric bulbs. On a misty evening the entire structure resembled an enchanted ship.

This happy summer crowd in 1927 had no idea that the Shelton Baths and the Colonial Theatre would be destroyed in an autumn fire.

The year 1901 was distinguished by several significant, historic events. On January 22 at age eighty-one, Queen Victoria of England died peacefully, ending a reign of almost sixty-four years, the longest in British history. A more violent change of government occurred that same year in the United States, when President William McKinley was assassinated on September 6, while visiting the Pan-American Exposition in Buffalo, New York. In the world of science, Guglielmo Marconi received the first transatlantic wireless message on December 12 in Newfoundland, setting the stage for modern communications, and on February 6, in Havana, Major Walter Reed reported the results of his research on the etiology of yellow fever, which led to the near eradication of this devastating disease.

The *Sindia* became forever bound to Ocean City when the four-masted, steel-hulled bark struck the shoals off of the beach on December 15, 1901. The ill-fated ship was heading for New York City from Japan when a brutal, four-day gale ended its sailing days.

The Wreck of the *Sindia*

In business in 1901 fortunes were still being amassed by the robber barons, but on January 10 the Standard Oil Trust czar, John D. Rockefeller, would have his luck turn in two unrelated events. The first took place in Beaumont, Texas, where a field that had been abandoned by Standard Oil as unproductive exploded with so much force it took over nine days to bring the well under control. Standard Oil executives watched in disbelief as the robust well produced over 110,000 barrels of oil per day. The Spindletop gusher eventually established Texas as the kingdom of black gold.

News of the second blow came from the quiet seaside town of Ocean City, New Jersey: the wreck of the *Sindia*, a 3,068-ton, 329-foot, four-masted, steel-hulled bark, one of the largest sailing vessels on the seas, and owned by John D. Rockfeller. The ill-fated ship began its voyage in New York City, sailed to Shanghai, China—where it discharged its original cargo—and headed to Japan to take on silks, oil, decorative screens, and porcelain. The estimated declared value of the goods was more than $1 million. The *Sindia* was a fine sailing vessel, built in the same Belfast, Ireland, shipyard that would later construct the *Titanic*. The ship's commander, Allen McKenzie, was a competent and experienced master who skillfully guided the *Sindia* around the treacherous waters of Cape Horn and followed the familiar shipping lanes to his destination, New York City. However, as he approached Cape May, New Jersey, he encountered a horrific gale that battered the *Sindia* for four days with up to 70-mile-per-hour winds and mountainous seas. McKenzie knew what a gale of this ferocity could do if

The Excursion House, the first amusement facility in Ocean City, was built in 1887. The building was located on the beach at 11th Street and provided all the amenities for "shoobies" (day-trippers) such as bathhouses, food, entertainment, and even bathing suits for rent by the hour. The first elevated boardwalk can be seen in front of the building. The Excursion House was destroyed by fire in 1900.

The Excursion House provided the first amusement ride in Ocean City. Pictured here is the very unique Elevated Bicycle ride. The earliest attractions were quite primitive and in this case self-powered.

his ship should wander too close to shore. On December 15 the commander lost the battle and came aground at low tide on a sandbar off Ocean City, parallel to 16th and 17th Streets. Each successive round of gale-force winds drove the doomed ship farther inland, until an unmistakable sound rose above the wind's fury, a sound that every sailor dreads and recognizes as his vessel's death toll—the sound of the hull splitting open. The victorious Atlantic immediately filled the *Sindia* with sand and seawater. Within two hours there was 9 feet of water in the hold. It was now just a matter of time. Distress flares were fired in rapid succession, and the thirty-three weary, wind-soaked crewmen were rescued by the fearless members of the Ocean City U.S. Life-Saving Service.

Although this wreck was an accident, it was not unusual for a scoundrel to tie a lantern to a donkey's tail, and to walk the animal up and down the coastline in bad weather. A sea captain who was attempting to ride out a storm would interpret the lantern as another ship, sail too close to shore, and break apart on a sandbar. "Pickens" was an age-old tradition along seacoast towns, and for two days, once the seamen were safely brought ashore, many a local helped himself to some of the *Sindia*'s precious cargo. Exotic shops featuring *Sindia* goods began appearing along the busy boardwalk. Many a coastal home was furnished with "pickens," a practice that died as Life Saving Stations, and eventually the U.S. Coast Guard, were created. The emergence of lighthouses also helped put an end to this deplorable practice.

Two days after the *Sindia* met her fate, the owner sent barges and salvage ships from New York City to rescue what cargo remained, but many think there is still treasure on board. That same day, a U.S. Customs officer was dispatched to the site, and for four years the shipwreck was patrolled as it sank deeper and deeper each year into the sand. One of the *Sindia*'s four masts was still visible from the Ocean City boardwalk when the Great Atlantic Hurricane of 1944 reduced it to a stump. In the Great Atlantic Storm of 1962, the *New York Times* reported that

"the storm uncovered quite a section of the bark *Sindia* which was driven ashore in 1901, and the vessel is becoming a local tourist sight."

What secrets did the *Sindia* take to the bottom? Some say that the vessel's manifest, which indicated that the hold of the square-rigged windjammer was filled with woven matting, manganese ore, bamboo, and 3,310 cases of curios, was not entirely accurate, nor entirely recovered. The first few years of salvage after the *Sindia* sunk produced several pieces of fine ivory and porcelain. One theory is that when the vessel unloaded a cargo of kerosene at Shanghai and took on 700 tons of stone ballast, it may have actually taken on valuable ivory and stone carvings as part of that ballast. A local legend that

will not die tells of a solid gold statue of Buddha smuggled aboard and never recovered. The wreck was eventually buried in 1991, when an Army Corps of Engineers' sand-replenishment project extended the strand more than 100 feet past where the ship broke apart. A marker on the Ocean City boardwalk indicates its location, alerting strollers of that December day more than a century ago and the treasures that may still lie beneath the sand.

From Camp Meetings to Resort

Just eleven years before the wreck of the *Sindia*, Ocean City did not exist. The new town, like Ocean Grove to the

Above: In order for a resort to prosper, it was necessary to supply reliable transportation. This train, known affectionately by the locals as the "Yellow Kid," ran between Stone Harbor and Ocean City. This photo was taken at the Stone Harbor terminal. Note the "cow-chaser" on the front of the engine.

Right: U.S. Life-Saving Servicemen during a practice drill on the Ocean City beach circa 1890. The focus of their attention is a short-barreled canon, or line-throwing gun, which was used in shore-based operations to launch a rescue line to the distressed ship. Breeches buoy equipment (a lifebuoy with canvas "breeches" for carrying the victim) was then relayed to the ship to facilitate the removal of ship's crew.

north, was created as a Methodist resort. In 1879 two clergymen, William B. Wood of Philadelphia and S. Wesley Lake of New Jersey, attended a camp meeting in Ocean Grove. They left the service with a dream of establishing their own religious seaside paradise founded on strict Methodist principles somewhere in southern New Jersey. Lake discussed the plan with his brothers, Ezra B. and James E. Lake, also Methodist ministers. The group appealed to the patriarch of the clan, the Honorable Simon Lake, a state legislator and prominent landowner, to bless their scheme and assist them with seed money for the ambitious venture. The Lake brothers, along with Wood and their business associate, William Burrell, had decided to purchase the wilderness barrier island of Peck's Beach on the Jersey keys to establish the island as a Christian sanctuary and resort. Simon Lake approved his boys' idea and raised the necessary funds by mortgaging his farm in Pleasantville, New Jersey, for $10,000.

Like Ludlam's Island, where Sea Isle City was established in 1880, and the rest of the Jersey keys, Peck's Beach was used from colonial days primarily as a place for cattle grazing, fishing, and whaling. Archaeological records indicate that Native Americans fished and whaled on the same island. Just before the Civil War, a

remote outpost here was used by Parker Miller, an insurance company representative, to assist ships in distress in the years before government-sponsored life-saving units were established.

On October 20, 1879, the Lake brothers, along with Wood and Burrell, met in Philadelphia to form their new association and to name their island paradise New Brighton, after the famous English resort. Just thirty days later, probably out of respect for Ocean Grove, the Methodist community model already on the northern Jersey shore, or perhaps when some pious potential lot owner pointed out that Brighton was not a "dry" town, they changed the name to Ocean City. The group issued stock and went to work laying out a city where there had been only sand and wilderness. Streets and avenues were established, and lots were surveyed. Just as James Bradley named his resort Asbury Park after the first Methodist bishop in the United States, the religious Lake brothers named a main thoroughfare in their fair city Asbury Avenue. But to guarantee that Ocean City's foundation as a religious haven would be built on more than just sand, they obtained title to every inch of Peck's Beach, incorporated their religious covenant restrictions into all deeds, and then went about selling the lots. Their covenants prohibited the sale or manufacture of

The Casino Pier was built in 1900 and stretched more than 700 feet from the boardwalk over the Atlantic. The casino, which could seat more than 2,000 people, was the location for the first Ocean City Baby Show. The pier was sold to John Lake Young in 1904.

The Hippodrome Pier and Theatre was the most popular amusement location on the boardwalk. The theater provided vaudeville acts and, later, moving photoplays. A dance pavilion was also provided, along with decking around three sides of the massive structure for sunbathing or people-watching. At one time the pier was called "The Ocean City Steeple Chase Pier," indicating it licensed the name and several rides from Coney Island Steeplechase innovator George Tilyou. A sign over the three arches to the left of the entrance reads DENTZEL'S CAROUSEL, in reference to one of the many hand-carved masterpieces that graced the Jersey Shore in the late nineteenth century.

alcoholic beverages and a no-commerce rule on the Sabbath. Although the Sunday restrictions have been relaxed, the resort of Ocean City is still a "dry" town. (Naturally, consuming alcohol in the privacy of a home is not restricted.) Urban legend states that some of the busiest liquor stores in the county are the ones that border Ocean City.

The association constructed a wharf to accommodate boats on the bay side, as well as an access road from the wharf to the city center. Campgrounds for religious meetings were created, and in August 1880 the first camp meeting took place over a ten-day period. The faithful pitched their tents—more than 1,000 Methodists attended the historic event. Following Ocean Grove's example, the Ocean City Association began building small, unassuming cottages for future

camp meetings and an auditorium for services and sermons. A finely appointed hotel across from the grounds stood ready for the less humble of the flock. The resort was an immediate success; by 1880 more than 500 private lots were sold.

"If you build it, they will come" may be accurate, but "they" also need a way to get there. In order to protect their investment, for the association was not adverse to turning a profit, the community leaders knew that the key to growth was reliable, comfortable transportation to their city from Atlantic City and, more importantly, Philadelphia. The Pleasantville and Ocean City Rail Road was established to transport eager prospects from Pleasantville to Somers Point. Being devout Methodists did not mean that the Lake boys and their friends were not competent businessmen, so on the railroad's first

Top: The Music Pavilion and Bowling Casino in 1910. The pavilion had decking on three sides so the public could practice the ageless activity of people-watching. The Bowling Casino is draped in flag bunting for a major holiday.

Left: A 1908 view of the Music Pavilion. The Music Pavilion led a charmed life. It escaped the great boardwalk fire of 1927 and was then moved to 6th Street, where it served as the city's Convention Hall until it was lost in a fire in 1965.

Right: A rare view of the Music Pavilion being moved to its new location at 6th Street, when the boardwalk was rebuilt closer to the ocean after the fire of 1927.

This wonderful image of families enjoying the Ocean City boardwalk over ninety years ago shows Foggs Pier, a popular boardwalk location, and Candy Land ice-cream cones available for 5 cents.

day of operation, free excursions were provided from Philadelphia to Ocean City. Another key component of a fledging resort was a barnlike structure, where room and board was provided for the trainloads of prospective lot buyers arriving daily. That building traditionally became the city's first hotel, once enough lots had been purchased. In the case of Ocean City, this was the Ocean House Hotel, later changed to the Brighton Hotel (someone in town still had a thing for Brighton). Not unlike today's time-share sales model, dinner was supplied for everyone who had the wherewithal to purchase a lot. The association also provided transportation from Somers Point to their island via a steamboat they had purchased. It docked five times a day at the wharf on 4th Street. In 1884, when the West Jersey and Seashore Railroad connected Sea Isle City with Ocean City, it was no longer necessary to take the ferry.

The major difference between the Jersey Shore's two Methodist resorts, Ocean Grove and Ocean City—besides approximately 70 miles—was that the Lake brothers and company did not attempt to govern their city in perpetuity as a religious resort. The association, as a private enterprise, governed Ocean City from its creation in 1879 until 1884, when the resort was incorporated into a borough complete with a mayor and four councilmen. In 1897 the resort was incorporated again, only this time into a city.

While the liquor prohibition has remained in place as part of the deed covenant restrictions, the Sunday sea-bathing ban was challenged and eliminated in the late nineteenth century. Likewise the Sabbath driving ban was no longer enforced. There was money to be made—and what would the city do with a trainload of tourists arriving on the Sunday special?

The Early Boardwalk

Although Ocean City was a dry town, it did not frown upon amusements. Records show the first boardwalk was constructed just about a year after the association was incorporated by an itinerate carpenter brought to the island to help build cottages and hotels. As with most new resorts, this walkway was portable and moved from the dunes to higher grounds each autumn. This first walkway was built between 4th and 7th Streets. Two meaningful events took place in 1887. The first was the extension of the boardwalk to 11th Street. The second was the construction of the resort's first amusement facility, the Excursion House, at the boardwalk and 11th Street. Excursion houses were traditionally built by the railroads eager to promote train travel for day-trippers. They usually provided bathhouses, restaurants, and amusements but not overnight accommodations. Here a "shoobie" could even rent bathing robes and towels by the hour.

One of Ocean City's first amusement attractions was sponsored by the Excursion House. Called the Elevated Bicycle, this high-tech nineteenth-century amusement ride consisted of wooden tracks elevated about 10 feet off the beach, with a series of bicycle-like contraptions hanging from them. A set of two oversize wheels rolled along the tracks above the riders, transporting them as they pedaled to their heart's content. A carousel and swings were also offered for the more faint of heart. Sadly, the Excursion House also provided the residents and tourists of Ocean City with another familiar seaside experience—fire. The facility burned to the ground in 1900.

Another scourge of seaside towns, the northeaster, struck Ocean City in 1888 and shredded the fragile boardwalk. This storm was known as the Great Blizzard of 1888, which crippled the eastern coast from Virginia to Maine from March 11 to 14. Almost 3 feet of snow fell in Ocean City, with hurricane-force winds tearing through the streets.

Around the turn of the century came the Ocean City Electric Railway Company, or the "Toonerville Trolley," as it was named by locals after a popular contemporary cartoon strip. Running from 1st to 59th Streets, it became a favorite means of transportation. For just 10 cents residents and tourists alike could travel to the remote section of the island on the open-air "Toonerville." With a combination of zigzagging tracks, clanking bells,

Above: Disaster struck Ocean City on October 11, 1927, when a mysterious fire did more than $2 million worth of damage to the famous wooden walkway. This view shows 9th Street and the boardwalk, where much of the damage occurred. More than thirty buildings, including the wonderful Hippodrome Pier and Theatre, were lost in the fire.

Below: After the fire the city immediately began construction of a new boardwalk several hundred feet closer to the Atlantic Ocean. The walkway was the first in the country to be constructed of concrete beams and pilings. Fir and spruce were the woods of choice for the beautiful new promenade.

and wide-track areas where passing motormen traveling north and south would decide who went first (sort of a nineteenth-century version of "chicken"), the old "Toonerville" gave the boardwalk amusement rides a run for their money. The tourist population of Ocean City further expanded with the addition of the Shore Fast Line, where riders could travel between Atlantic City and Ocean City.

Pleasing the Crowds

After the 1888 storm wrecked the boardwalk, a raised, "permanent" walkway was built the following year from 7th to 13th Streets. The next year saw the addition of pavilions and bathhouses. By this era entrepreneurs realized that the sand that surrounded the walkway was golden, and every inch of the walkway was used to part passersby from their nickels and dimes. Bathhouses added shooting galleries or shuffleboard games to supplement their earnings from renting "sanitized bathing robes and towels" by the hour. And there was always a popular fad of the day to bring out the tourists. In the late nineteenth and early twentieth centuries, for example, "mock trials" were held on the boardwalks up and down the Jersey Shore. (Cap May "tried" the mayor for installing lights on the boardwalk and putting an end to evening "spooning." The young girls of the town played the role of the prosecutors.)

Photo studios and postcard shops began appearing along the boardwalk, and for a nickel, a souvenir image of Ocean City could be purchased to mail home. It did not take long for an enterprising postcard manufacturer to understand that a unique image would sell at each shore location by just changing the name. While collecting images for this book, I came across the same circa 1910 postcard of a beached whale with a crowd of men, women, and children crowded around the stricken beast. The caption reads ENORMOUS WHALE WASHED ASHORE. The only difference is that each card has a

The Ocean City Music Pier, a Spanish revival building, was constructed in 1928–29 after the fire and remains an Ocean City landmark. Located at Moorlyn Terrace, it is the venue for summer concerts, musicals, crafts shows, and other community activities.

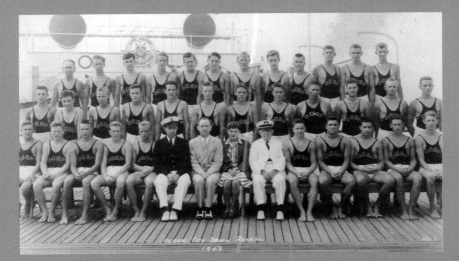

The Kelly family spent their summers in Ocean City. John Kelly achieved fame before his daughter Grace (right) became world famous as an Academy Award–winning actress and the Princess of Monaco. A world-class crew athlete, in 1920 he won two Olympic gold medals in Belgium in the sculls racing and won the gold again in Paris in 1924. The Kellys summered at their home at 26th Street across from the ocean. John's son, Jack Jr. (left; back row, fourth from right) was an Ocean City lifeguard and won the Beach Patrol and South Jersey championships as an oarsman.

different resort name under the caption. Apparently this poor leviathan had died in the same position surrounded by the same crowd on the same summer day at Asbury Park, Atlantic City, Ocean City, Long Branch, and Wildwood.

Piers were always the rage. The promoter need only purchase the rights to the boardwalk entrance, and he could build his wooden dynasty as far out to sea as his wallet and nature would allow. One such pier made its debut in Ocean City in 1900. Called the Casino Pier, with an entrance at 9th Street and the boardwalk, it stretched seaward more than 700 feet. Its massive casino had a seating capacity of more than 2,000 people. The Casino Pier became an instant hit, as people whiled away the endless summer season at dances, concerts, and the ever-popular Baby Show, later a parade, when the casino could no longer hold the burgeoning crowds. Like most boardwalk piers, the Casino Pier was outlined with hundreds of electric bulbs, the latest technology of the era. On a misty evening the entire structure would take on the appearance of an enchanted sea vessel. This was where most Ocean City visitors and residents got their first glimpse of the stricken ship *Sindia* as it ran aground

in 1901. In 1904 the Casino Pier was sold to John Lake Young, who also made his mark developing a pier in Atlantic City, and renamed Young's Pier.

In the spring of 1905, the city marked the debut of its wider, 2-mile-long boardwalk with a daylong celebration complete with a crowd-pleasing parade. That summer also marked the completion of the Municipal Music Pavilion, located at 8th Street and the boardwalk, Ocean City's first public facility on the ocean side of the boardwalk. It cost approximately $10,000 to build the spacious public auditorium, band shell, and roomy solarium furnished with wicker rockers, where the public could spend a perfectly beautiful summer afternoon or evening listening to free concerts by the popular bands of the day. Across from the Music Pavilion stood the Bowling Casino, with bowling alleys on the ground floor and a Casino Club on the second. (The casino advertised itself as a respite from the tumult of the busy wooden walkway, though one wonders about the level of sound emanating from the alleys below.) The club was not too exclusive—members could join by the day, week, month, or season. By 1915 the boardwalk extended from 2nd to 13th Streets, and the Baby Show had evolved into the

Baby Parade, complete with a Queen Infante and Royal Court.

Another important addition to the boardwalk's ever-evolving collection of bathhouses, bowling alleys, and concessions (such as Shriver's Candy, a local favorite) was the massive Hippodrome Pier, located at the boardwalk and Moorlyn Terrace on land previously used by Young's Pier. Alongside stood the Hippodrome Theatre, later named the Strand. This was the most popular amusement complex in Ocean City, offering a hand-carved Dentzel carousel as well as other rides, a dance pavilion, vaudeville "photoplays" (two shows every Saturday night, with a 3:00 P.M. matinee), and a colossal open deck at the end of the pier. By 1913 it was also referred to as the Ocean City Steeple Chase Pier, a brand licensed from George Tilyou, the Coney Island, New York, amusement impresario who had invented many of the popular attractions of the day. Tilyou's signature attraction gave eager patrons the excitement of horse racing via riding ornate wooden horses along a set of parallel rolling tracks. Another Tilyou favorite was the Human Roulette Wheel, where men and women rode atop a large spinning wheel that eventually deposited

them into a pile of humanity on the deck below. Part of Tilyou's genius lay in realizing that—in an era when the sexes followed rigid rules for fraternizing—the boardwalk experience allowed for a suspension of those mores, if only for just a few hours. He even provided a game where for 25 cents the player could throw balls at neatly stacked—very cheap—ceramic tableware. The sign read IF YOU CAN'T BREAK THEM AT HOME, BREAK THEM HERE.

Mysterious Fires

The 1927 summer season ended in the usual manner. Shops closed, hotels sent their staff home, and the wooden walkway prepared to ride out another winter on the Jersey Shore. But on October 11 a mysterious fire started under the boardwalk at the corner of 9th Street. Within minutes the fire spread a block each way north and south and then headed inland, fanned by a powerful ocean wind. The conflagration destroyed almost everything in its path and was not stopped until it had advanced five avenues inland and came face to face with the more modern fireproof buildings along Asbury Avenue, the resort's main business district. Reports

From the humble Gillian's Fun Deck (left) grew today's Gillian's Wonderland Pier (right) empire that now operates some of Ocean City's most exciting amusements.

later came in that the inferno lit the October night sky for a 25-mile radius.

By the time the monstrous fire was subdued, it had claimed thirty buildings and a financial toll over $2 million. Amazingly, there was no loss of life. The beach took on the appearance of a makeshift tag sale as property owners, with the assistance of the Boy Scouts, spent the evening piling merchandise, bedding, personal property, furniture, and other items just beyond the high-water mark and out of the path of the fire. The city posted policemen along the beach, as some looting had already

occurred. Lost in the fire were 500 feet of boardwalk from 9th to 10th Streets, the Hippodrome pier and theater, the Arcadia building and its concessions, Shriver's Candy, McFarland's Shooting Gallery, Seaside Baths, the Colonial Theater, the Shelton Baths, two large hotels, and scores of smaller buildings.

There is always the possibility of arson when a boardwalk fire takes place after the season ends, but no one was ever charged with starting this blaze, and the city adopted a new building code and set to work rebuilding the old walkway several hundred feet closer to the ocean.

Above: A view of the Hippodrome Theatre and Shriver's Candy before the Great Boardwalk Fire of 1927 turned this section of the Ocean City boardwalk into a pile of ashes.

Right: The Shore Fast Line provided service between Ocean City and Atlantic City. Here, passengers are boarding the train at the 8th Street Terminal in Ocean City. The trolley ran on the hour and provided service until World War II.

The new boardwalk, built at a cost of just under $250,000, was the first in the United States to be constructed of concrete beams, with the new boards and supports made from California redwood and Washington State fir. Other changes also took place: The old Music Pavilion was moved from Moorlyn Terrace to 6th Street and given a new life as the city's Convention Hall. It remained the center of community activities and political rallies until it too was lost in a fire in 1965. Oddly, Doughty's Pier and Theater now faced inland, as the new boardwalk met what had been the ocean end of the pier. It was resurrected as the Village Theatre at 8th Street and the new walkway.

Just six months after the first fire, a smaller blaze did $100,000 damage to the walkway. This one was determined to be arson, as it started simultaneously at 3:00 A.M. on both sides of 8th Street. Lost were the Doughty Building, ten stores, and seven other structures. The fire was discovered by a watchman for the Bader Construction Company, the firm building the new boardwalk. The newspapers reported that the mayor had recently received a letter threatening his and the lives of the other city commissioners should a proposed mercantile tax go into effect. Apparently, the author meant business.

America's Greatest Family Resort

Coincidentally, the 1927 fire set into motion a series of events that would create the Gillian amusement empire on the wooden walkway. David Gillian had enjoyed several summer seasons playing drums in an orchestra at the Hippodrome Pier and Theatre. When the fire destroyed that landmark building, he found himself out of a job. As a boy in Easton, Pennsylvania, Gillian had worked for a short while in a local amusement park and was enamored with its magical hand-carved carousel. This prompted the unemployed musician to convince the owner of a miniature-golf course along the Ocean City boardwalk to lease him space to operate a merry-go-round. He bought a used carousel and eventually established Gillian's Fun Deck. Both of David Gillian's sons, Roy and Rob, joined the family business, and as time passed, Roy broke off on his own to start a new ven-

A typical boardwalk game during the early 1930s. The Sherwood Forest range was 20 yards, with targets that varied in size from 16 to 24 inches. Deck chairs were provided for spectators.

ture. He purchased the old site of Stainton's Playland, an amusement park destroyed by fire in 1955. This acquisition was the beginning of Gillian's Wonderland Pier, one of the most famous boardwalk amusement operations in New Jersey.

Rides and attractions came and went over the decades, as the public's taste in entertainment continued to evolve. A hand-carved, forty-five-horse Dentzel carousel was sold off in the 1960s because the public wanted merry-go-rounds where the figures went up and

down. The Gillians' goal was to keep the people coming by staying one step ahead of the competition. In 1989 they acquired the Giant Ferris Wheel that has become an Ocean City landmark, visible from the Garden State Parkway. It provides a magnificent view of the Atlantic and Ocean City. Today the Gillian family offers three main Ocean City boardwalk staples: Gillian's Wonderland Pier, Gillian's Island Waterpark, and Gillian's Island Adventure Golf. These, along with many other attractions and events, earn Ocean City its trade-marked slogan: America's Greatest Family Resort.

Sea Isle City

Known by many as "the city that refuses to quit," Sea Isle City has stubbornly stood up to the Atlantic's fury time after time, refusing to give in. As recently as 1991, a Halloween storm flooded the city and carried away most of the resort's recently replenished beach.

Enjoying the surf in Sea Isle City in 1906. The Excursion House can be seen in the upper left. This photograph shows the scale of the resort's famous strand before the Great Atlantic Storm of 1962 altered it forever.

While touring Italy in 1872, Charles Landis visited Venice and marveled at the classical architecture and the historic city's system of canals and lagoons. Landis had achieved fame in the United States in 1861 as the founder of Vineland, a community carved out of the Pine Barrens of New Jersey. He laid out his ideal city in a square, precisely 1 mile on each side. Landis insisted on temperance and a hardy prescription of industry and agriculture from the new citizens of Vineland, many of them Italian immigrants whom he had persuaded to migrate to his utopian community.

Landis had more than sightseeing on his mind as he wandered the narrow streets of Venice. A year before this inspirational trip abroad, he had been driven to distraction by a series of articles written by Uri Carruth, the outspoken editor of the *Vineland Independent* newspaper. The no-nonsense founder of the pastoral community apparently decided the newspaper was a bit too independent, and he walked over to its office and shot Carruth in the back of the head. The unfortunate editor lingered on for seven months, but eventually succumbed to the gunshot wound.

An aerial view from 1950 provides a glimpse of Charles Landis's dream of creating a Venice along the Jersey Shore. While additional canals exist today, the original plan never materialized.

The Landis defense was simple. "'Twas true, I murdered Carruth most foully, but just at that particular moment I was insane," Landis testified at his trial in Bridgeton, New Jersey. "There is nothing wrong with me, and I want to improve my property and Vineland." Witnesses were produced to testify that Landis was most certainly deranged when he pulled the trigger. King Landis, as he was known by his enemies, hired seven attorneys, and it appears he received good value for his money, since he was acquitted. After the jury found him innocent, the judge stated for the record that Landis was sane before the murder and most certainly sane when he appeared in court, so therefore the insanity had to be temporary. Charles Landis was set free, and went abroad.

Venice on the Jersey Shore

On his return to the United States, Landis set his sights on establishing a version of Venice along the Jersey coast. He chose one of the keys (low islands) in Cape May County for his seaside paradise, and in 1880 purchased Ludlam's Island, named after Joseph Ludlam, one of Cape May County's original settlers. Just as Vineland became a viable community when the railroad from Camden to Glassboro was extended to Millville,

The resort's wooden walkway in the early twentieth century. This was the era when people dressed in their "Sunday best" to promenade the boardwalk. Bathing suits were for the beach only.

A later view of the boardwalk looking south from 43rd Street.

Landis knew that the then-desolate wasteland of Ludlam's Island, with its 6½-mile beach, would flourish with the completion of a proposed railroad spur. The Sea Isle City Improvement Company was organized to promote the property and attract cottagers, and by 1881 a published map of "Sea Isle City, Ludlam Island, New Jersey" advertised 5,405 surveyed lots, indicating the majority of the beachfront lots as well as numerous interior lots as already sold.

Additional growth came in 1882, when the Ocean City Railroad Company ran a 4.8-mile line from the West Jersey Railroad's Cape May line to provide first-class service to Sea Isle City. Further expansion came in 1897, when the Ocean City Railroad became part of the South Jersey Railroad, creating a valuable link to Philadelphia through Winslow Junction. In just seventeen years the community grew from a small town of one hotel and a dozen homes to a popular resort with thirty stately hotels and more than three hundred houses. So promising were its prospects that its chief engineer wrote in a company report: "With proper railroad facilities, and lots offered at a reasonable price, I do not see why this place

should not become as great a resort as Atlantic City." His optimism had firm grounding on the quality of the Sea Isle City beach and the fact that a vacationer from Philadelphia could reach Sea Isle in the same amount of time as Atlantic City. The railroad would eventually connect the Jersey keys from Ocean City to Wildwood, bringing along with it an influx of investors and tourists.

Landis named his Venice on the Jersey Shore Sea Isle City, and it quickly became a favorite of the Philadelphia elite. He planned to build a series of canals and lagoons and Venetian-style fountains and public baths, and to adorn the city with classical statues, artwork, and Renaissance-style public buildings. In 1893 the innovative founder introduced brilliant electric lights to the city and boardwalk; small pavilions along the popular walkway followed. In 1889 the grand Continental Hotel was built on the beach between 25th and 26th Streets, with a boardwalk extending from the hotel to the center of the resort. The five-story Continental offered all of the amenities of the era, including the only steam-powered elevator in Cape May County.

The entrance to the Sea Isle City Ocean Pier when it opened in 1906.

The Fishing Pier located off 42nd Street and the boardwalk as it looked circa 1915. When the tide was in, the pier gave fishermen the feeling of being on a boat out to sea. The pier was a victim of the Great Atlantic Storm of 1962.

Once a railroad connected a resort to a busy metropolis such as Philadelphia, it was necessary to provide a building for the "shoobies," or excursionists. These visitors took advantage of the faster train connections to spend a day at the beach and return home on a late-night train. Many traveled with their lunch in a shoebox tucked under their train seat—hence the name "shoobie." While the hotel owners were not fond of these new day-vacationers, "shoobies" were a reality, and Jersey Shore entrepreneurs realized that there was money to be made by catering to them as well. They needed a place to change, relax, and enjoy a meal because they were not staying overnight at a hotel or guesthouse. Many rented bathing suits just for the afternoon. The Landis family constructed a three-story building to suit these needs in 1892—the Sea Isle City Excursion House. Here daily visitors enjoyed an indoor hardwood roller-skating rink, an observation deck, and even a top-floor ballroom that hosted hops, talent shows, orchestra music, and the occasional prizefight. The Excursion House quickly became the center of public events for the resort.

In 1905, a year before the first boardwalk was constructed, the Sea Isle Yacht and Motor Club was organized, and a pier quickly followed. Known as the Ocean Pier and leading out from the foot of 41st and 42nd Streets, it was primarily a fishing pier. By 1915 residents and tourists could avail themselves of a trolley line that paralleled the ocean from Avalon to Ocean City. The Sea Isle City boardwalk was washed away in 1928 and was reconstructed a few years later. Unfortunately, this was just the first skirmish between the wooden walkway and the hungry Atlantic, as the city suffered a number of destructive storms and lost a series of boardwalks. When the Great Atlantic Storm of 1962 wiped out the entire beachfront of the city, it, like Cape May to the south, gave up the boardwalk ghost. This time, Sea Isle City constructed a dune line, strengthened it with heavy boulders, and topped the seawall off with a bituminous asphalt promenade. The tiny resort had suffered horrific damage as the Atlantic Ocean covered the city and merged with the bay for several hours. The fishing pier was a victim of the 1962 storm, along with the historic

Excursion House. Also lost was a beautiful hand-carved carousel manufactured by the Philadelphia craftsman William Dentzel. Known by the locals simply as "the merry-go-round," almost all of the handcrafted animals were plowed into the sand and debris left by the storm as the bulldozer operators attempted to construct a temporary barrier to stop the tidal damage. For years, town historians have unsuccessfully searched for surviving carousel animals that they believe may be in the hands of a few collectors. Unbelievable as it may sound, the town historical society has also been unable to locate a photo of the actual carousel—all that survives is a photo of the building after the storm. This is not an unusual occurrence. "Why take a photo of the merry-go-round?" most people felt at the time. "It isn't going anywhere." Mother Nature had a different plan in mind.

Today Sea Isle City is a summer cottage community with a small boardwalk amusement center, Fun City. Condominiums near the water attest to the city's continued popularity. Known by many as "the city that refuses to quit," it has stood up to the Atlantic's fury time after time without yielding. As recently as 1991, a Halloween storm (responsible for more than $90 million of damage at the Jersey Shore) flooded the city and carried away most of the recently replenished beach.

Charles Landis's dream of creating a Venice on the Jersey Shore never materialized. The railroad connection proved to be a two-edged sword, providing access to the other fledgling resorts along the Jersey keys, as well as Sea Isle City. The resulting competition for Philadelphia cottagers drove down the price of the Sea Isle City lots. It

The Continental Hotel was the first hotel along the New Jersey coast to provide steam elevators for its guests. The boardwalk extended from the center of Sea Isle City to the front of the Continental. The hotel was razed in the early twentieth century.

MOTORCYCLE BATHING BEAUTY PRIZE

Beauty contests were a favorite on the Jersey boardwalks, and this one took place in Sea Isle City in the early 1920s. By this time the heavy flannel bathing suits that covered a woman from her neck to her ankles had gone the way of the horse and carriage.

is not clear if or how many Venetian-style statues Landis purchased for his city, but none remain today. The best, most tantalizing glimpse of his original vision can be seen via an aerial view of the city's only canals that were actually dug and still exist, in the bayside section of Sea Isle City. But even though the planned-for classical public buildings were never constructed for lack of funds, the promenade remains a favorite location for a summertime stroll or the ubiquitous Jersey Shore surrey ride.

Wildwood

The tram cars that would become synonymous with the Wildwood boardwalk made their appearance in 1949, when local promoter S. B. Ramagosa purchased cars that had been used at the 1939 New York World's Fair. He charged one dime for a ride. The trams quickly eclipsed the older roller chairs.

Today the Wildwood boardwalk is the amusement center of the Jersey Shore, with Morey's Piers offering more than seventy rides, including seven roller coasters along with a first-class water park.

J ust after midnight on a still, moonlit early Sunday morning in 1920, a group of men quietly approached the Wildwood boardwalk. The concessions and rides were shut down for the evening, and only the rolling surf could be heard in the distance. Armed with sledgehammers and axes, they went to work dismantling a section of the wooden walkway at a feverish pitch. By daybreak all that remained were the pilings where it once stood. Was this a group of madmen? Perhaps some devilish band of pranksters? Not likely. One of the men had even brought along his eleven-year-old son to help. Armed with his trusty Boy Scout hatchet, the boy whacked at the boardwalk along with his father and the makeshift group of hired hands.

The boy's father was city commissioner Oliver Bright, and he timed his assault knowing that no judge in rural Cape May County could be found on a Sunday to prevent them from dismantling the boardwalk. The event was a culmination of an acrimonious dispute between the city government and the merchants and landowners who depended on the Wildwood boardwalk for their livelihood. At first glance, the walkway appeared to be a wonderful success, with crowds growing each season and the railroad adding more first-class cars to carry the hoards of sea lovers to the popular resort. The merchants were selling more and more popcorn, root beer, candy apples, and souvenirs, and the bathhouses were packed every weekend. So what was the problem?

A view of the Ocean Pier following movie theater mogul William C. Hunt's purchase of the landmark in 1935. By the time this photograph was taken, Hunt had added the Funchase giant slide to the pier, a concept he borrowed from Coney Island amusement impresario George Tilyou. Another popular attraction was the Human Roulette wheel, which was guaranteed to start a conversation between the men and women on board.

Bright and other commissioners realized that a new boardwalk had to be built closer to the ever-expanding Wildwood beach. The current one was in need of repair, and the trek from the boardwalk to the ocean at low tide was getting longer each season. This was nothing new—the resort had been forced to move a series of more primitive walkways throughout its history as the beach grew each year. But this time the stakes were higher. The busy merchants did not want to lose their profitable concessions, and the landowners wanted to protect their seaside—soon to become inland—lots. They fought as if their livelihood depended on it, which it did, and organized a recall election. Oliver Bright was eventually recalled from office, but not before his midnight raid. Some said he had ulterior motives and was involved in land speculation. No matter; he destroyed enough of the aging walkway that in 1921 a new section of boardwalk, one closer to the Atlantic Ocean, was completed from Cedar to Montgomery Avenues.

The Casino Pier, which opened in 1897, was the second pier to evolve from a Wildwood boardwalk pavilion. The view here is from the Casino's popular fishing pier, which extended hundreds of feet out to sea.

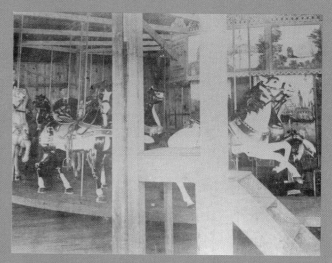

One of the major attractions at the Casino Pier in 1897 was its beautiful hand-carved carousel manufactured by Philadelphia craftsman Gustav A. Dentzel. At one time Dentzel carousels dotted the Jersey Shore, but today the only operating boardwalk machine is located in Seaside Heights, in a facility coincidently named Casino Pier.

Developing the Jersey Keys

In 1892, twenty-eight years before the Bright Battle of the Boardwalk, ornithologist Charles Abbott visited the fledgling resort of Wildwood during the waning days of the primeval wonderland that was the region's namesake. He feared that the area's reputation "as a relic of old New Jersey" might have been exaggerated, but was happy to later write of his visit, "I had found a wild-wood in the fullest sense of that suggestive phrase." Abbott marveled at the "scores of magnificent hollies" and was in awe of one specimen 68 inches in circumference and 40 feet high. He wrote of plants twisted in a variety of shapes, from corkscrews to exotic creatures: "Other hollies have assumed even animal-like shapes; the resemblance in one instance to an elephant's head and trunk being very marked." Perhaps these shapes were prophetic of the bizarre and colorful amusements that would someday line the town's 2½-mile cedar walkway.

The Wildwoods are located on a barrier island in the Jersey keys known as Five-Mile Beach. The nearby three barrier islands, separated from each other by deep inlets, were Peck's Beach (today Ocean City), Ludlam's Beach (now Sea Isle City), and Strathmere and Seven Mile Beach (now Stone Harbor and Avalon). The region was slow to develop, as it was separated from the mainland by a string of muddy marshes, saltwater channels, and treacherous sounds. Although Cape May on the southern end of the peninsula was a booming resort town of national renown, the barrier islands remained desolate, the seaside realm of a handful of cattlemen who grazed their herds on the salt hay and grasses. (The deep tidal inlets and marshes and channels acted as natural fences, confining the cattle to the individual islands.) The cattlemen were kept company by oystermen and whalers, as well as a handful of hardy men who manned the lifesaving stations located on the islands. The unforgiving seas off the Jersey keys were a graveyard for ships that wandered too close to the cape, or were driven inland by fierce northeasters. In 1848 the federal government created the Life Saving Service and established stations along the coast and on the Jersey keys. It was not until the late nineteenth century that developers

This circa 1900 view shows the second Wildwood boardwalk. The beach has expanded so much in the past hundred-plus years that the wooden walkway is now several blocks inland, at Atlantic Avenue. Also shown is the pavilion and fishing pier built by the Baker brothers in 1888. Latimer Baker, seen here in a straw hat, was elected Wildwood's first mayor in 1895.

and promoters took notice of the pristine white beaches of the barrier islands. The "key" to the Jersey keys' development turned out to be the railroads. The well-connected developers knew that proposed railway connections would soon carry thousands of Philadelphians to the barrier islands, and the first two resorts were created: Ocean City and Sea Isle City. John Burk, a partner and onetime clerk of Sea Isle City's colorful founder, Charles Landis, quarreled with Landis when the boss discovered his ambitious employee was planning his own resort. Burk had recently organized the Holly Beach Improvement Company with several investors to develop a first-class resort on Five-Mile Beach.

North of Holly Beach was the small fishing community of Anglesea, today North Wildwood. Development of this section of the Wildwoods began when the Anglesea Land Company was created in 1882, and lots were sub-

divided and offered to the public. Next was the Wildwood Beach Improvement Company, organized in 1885 by another former Landis partner, Philip P. Baker. Joined by brothers J. Thompson and Latimer, the Baker trio set out to develop the region between Anglesea and Holly Beach. Their first decision was what to call their new resort. They came close to choosing Florida City but eventually decided on Wildwood, after the primeval bramble that once occupied Five-Mile Beach.

In a short time cottages and hotels rose on the island, and the cattlemen and fishermen were replaced by herds of wealthy Philadelphians searching for an escape from clutter and pollution. Nineteenth-century cities were ripe with disease during the sweltering summer months, and the periodicals of the era espoused the health benefits of a dip in the refreshing Atlantic Ocean. As railroad connections improved and first-class travel became a reality, crowds also grew, as did the need for an amusement industry.

Wildwood Amusements

Records indicate that a small wooden walkway existed in Anglesea by 1884. It was no doubt used to connect the hotels along the beach and was probably stored away after the summer season. By 1893 Holly Beach also possessed a small boardwalk. It wasn't until 1899 that one of the Baker brothers, Latimer, by now the mayor of the Borough of Wildwood, supervised the construction of a 450-foot boardwalk on the sand from Atlantic Avenue to Maple Avenue. He also suggested that a series of small wooden "pagodas," or pavilions, be installed along the walkway.

During this era the resorts that comprised what today is known as the Wildwoods constructed a series of ever-expanding boardwalks independent of each community and always a bit closer to the ever-expanding beach-front. By 1900 another new walkway was built at Atlantic and Maple Avenues. The constant pounding of the waves wore away the fragile walkways, and an occasional northeaster transformed them into expensive kindling.

As the boardwalks evolved, so did many of the pavilions. Once a developer owned a pavilion, he was free to build as far out into the ocean as the technology of the era, and his fortune, would permit. The Wildwood beach was growing at a rate of 75 to 100 feet per year, providing plenty of opportunity to expand a pier. One of these early entrepreneurs was George H. Blaker, who in 1891 purchased a pier and began to build it farther out into the

Christened the Ocean Pier, the resort's first major pier opened in the 1905–06 season to compete with those in Atlantic City. Located on the boardwalk between Poplar and Juniper Avenues, the 1,000-foot pier cost $150,000 to build. It offered eight bowling alleys, a theater, a roller-skating rink, and a second-floor dance hall. As advertised on the tower to the right, the Ocean Pier had its own hand-carved carousel. There were hot and cold showers, bathhouses, and as a sign on the building boldly stated, BATHING ROBES TO HIRE.

The Ocean Pier's second-floor ballroom was a tremendous draw. It is seen here decorated with pennants and fanciful hanging lanterns. Bands from Philadelphia entertained tourists during the summer season.

In 1916 the owners of the Ocean Pier installed Wildwood's first roller coaster, the Yankee Dip. While it
appeared to be a success, a winter of bad weather along
with petty local politics doomed the coaster, which did
not open the following season. In 1919 Edward E. Rhoads
opened the wooden Jack Rabbit roller coaster on what
was known as Blaker Block, between Cedar and
Schellenger Avenues; it became an immediate success.

A detailed view of the Ed Rhoads Amusement Park
showing the carousel building on the left and the Jack
Rabbit roller coaster in the background. When the
boardwalk was moved in the 1920s, the Jack Rabbit
ended up on the inland side of the walkway.

surf. Horace Greeley may have previously advised a generation of ambitious easterners to "go west, young man,"
but the first boardwalk promoters knew their fortunes
lay on the eastern horizon. These ventures were not for
the weak of heart, as Blaker discovered when his new
pier was reduced to a mound of shattered cedar during a
storm in 1892. Undaunted by the challenge, Blaker
rebuilt a larger facility, complete with rudimentary
amusements and concessions. He also added bathhouses,
ice-cream parlors, a bandstand, and an auditorium that
evolved into Blaker's Theatre. The pier auditorium provided a venue for amateur stock companies and fashionable musicians of the era. Today local historians consider
Blaker to be the father of the Wildwood amusement pier.

The next pier to evolve from a boardwalk pavilion,
known as the Casino, opened for business in 1897. This
facility's fishing pier gave visitors the chance to view the
boardwalk from hundreds of feet out to sea. A major

attraction was the hand-carved, steam-powered
carousel created by famed craftsman Gustav A. Dentzel.
(At one time several Dentzel carousels dotted the New
Jersey coastline, but today the only surviving Dentzel
masterpiece is located at Casino Pier in Seaside Heights,
New Jersey.)

Wildwood's first major amusement pier was modeled
after the famous piers of Atlantic City. Wildwood recognized their wealthy neighbor to the north as the gold
standard of the amusement industry, and the early promoters dreamed of achieving the same success. The
1,000-foot-long Ocean Pier opened in the 1905–1906
season off Poplar and Juniper Avenues. It cost more than
$150,000 to construct and offered eight bowling alleys,
a theater, ballroom, roller-skating rink, second-floor
dance hall, and, of course, a hand-carved carousel,
complete with a pipe organ. Bathhouses were provided,
along with facilities for hot and cold sea bathing and

showers to wash off the sand after a refreshing dip in the Atlantic. A vaudeville theater and later a moving picture theater were also added. The promoters hired the best bands and orchestras from Philadelphia and New York City for concerts during the busy summer season. Novelty acts, including magicians, dancing dogs, and musical prodigies, were popular attractions. Refreshments included hot dogs; roasted peanuts; ice cream; lemonade; spruce, root, and birch beer; and a local favorite, Sagel's saltwater taffy. Thousands of multicolored incandescent lightbulbs outlined the massive structure, allowing the palace of fun to be seen for miles offshore.

The pier was also the site of Wildwood's first roller coaster, the Yankee Dip, locally known simply as Ocean Pier Coaster. While it looked like a winner and the crowds lined up with their money in hand, the coaster fell victim to bad weather and petty city politics and closed after only one season. Wildwood's second, more permanent roller coaster arrived when Edward E. Rhoads converted what was known as Blaker Block (between Cedar and Schellenger Avenues) into a first-class amusement park. Until then, most of Wildwood's amusements were of a smaller scale. Rhoads contracted with the famed Philadelphia Toboggan Company to construct a handmade carousel to match the Dentzel machine in beauty and quality. Next he set his eyes on a roller coaster, and by 1919 Wildwood saw the opening of the Jack Rabbit, a massive wooden roller coaster, along with the extremely popular Old Mill boat ride, a dark, early-twentieth-century version of a tunnel of love.

Within a few years Ocean Pier began to receive even more serious competition, as the Casino Pier expanded to include a roller-skating rink. The roller skate was to the early-twentieth-century Jersey Shore what the hula hoop was to the 1950s, with some facilities attracting huge crowds. Times were good for the Wildwood amusement business. New piers began to appear, including a small facility at Wildwood Crest known as the Crest Pier. Every pier needed a unique attraction, or gimmick, and the Crest Pier's claim to fame was the Mirror Maze.

Boardwalk merchants not only had to contend with the laws of nature, as evidenced by the storms that from time to time would batter their investments to pieces, but also with the laws of man. While some Jersey Shore resorts such as Ocean Grove and Ocean City had voluntarily passed their own "Never on Sunday" ordinances,

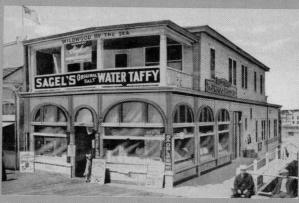

Bruce Minnix recalls the days he spent on the Wildwood boardwalk, and how on his twelfth birthday in 1935 he hitchhiked the 5 miles from his family home in Rio Grande to Wildwood. "It was a magic place," he remembers. "It had rides, ice-cream stands, games of chance, shops and movies." His first boardwalk job was picking up marbles at a Slingshot game, where people tried to win a stuffed animal by shooting marbles at a bell. When there were no customers, Bruce was permitted to practice, and he became quite proficient. In true boardwalk entrepreneurial style, his boss would give Bruce a dime and send him out the back door, where he would walk around the corner and approach the booth to draw a crowd. Bruce (who later became an Emmy Award–Winning director, producer, and writer) found he had a knack for playing to the gathering crowd. He would inquire about the game, ask about the prizes, and after a minute or two of instruction from the booth owner, he'd start ringing the bell. There'd be a line of people behind the youngster when he left the booth with his prize, a giant stuffed animal. The future showman would walk down the walkway, around the corner, and in the back door of the booth, where his boss would put the animal back on the shelf. As soon as the crowd had changed, Bruce would reappear and begin picking up the marbles again.

Pictured is the dapper young man on the Wildwood boardwalk in front of Sagel's Saltwater Taffy, located near the Ocean Pier at Poplar Avenue. Sagel's was lost in the Christmas Day fire of 1943.

Although most people associate rolling chairs with Atlantic City, they were a popular attraction on the Wildwood boardwalk before trams made their debut. The Blaker Brothers Rolling Chair Company became fashionable when the united boardwalks created a 2-mile walkway. A single chair rented for 25 cents an hour, and an attendant could be hired for another quarter.

The tram cars that would become synonymous with the Wildwood boardwalk made their appearance in 1949, when local promoter S. B. Ramagosa purchased units that had been used at the 1939 New York World's Fair. He charged one dime for a ride. This photograph was taken in 1979 in front of the old Sportland Pier, where the carousel was a favorite attraction with its colorful, beautifully hand-carved horses.

there existed laws on the state books from the eighteenth century that forbade, among many things, amusements on Sunday. Many a boardwalk pioneer spent a night in jail in defiance of the law. Enforcement varied, depending on the current moral temperature of the era, but the battle raged well into the late 1970s.

Another legal issue that plagued the region's boardwalks involved the question of games of chance versus games of skill—a distinction that often depended on how resort-friendly local officials were. From time to time a major antigambling initiative would shut down all of the wheels of fortune and boardwalk games of skill or chance, and certainly there were many instances of "fixed" games. In 1957 the fight went to the New Jersey State Supreme Court, where in a 6–1 decision games of skill became illegal. The court felt that as long as money was wagered, it did not matter whether the game required skill or chance. This decision dealt a serious blow to the boardwalks, as more than $100 million (in 1950s dollars) was generated that year by the industry.

The court cited as an example an old boardwalk staple, the "ring the bottle" game. The justices felt that, although the game was innocuous and offered "noncash" prizes, it was still gambling as defined in the state constitution. Three years later, driven by powerful New Jersey state senator Charles Sandman, a bill passed via a statewide referendum that established a strict licensing program and limited the type of games that could be played and the value of the prize. The boardwalk merchants were back in business, and "board rats" once again spent their dollars tossing a ring at soda bottles or throwing a dart at hanging balloons—perhaps taking home a prized stuffed animal worth about 50 cents.

The Ever-Changing Boardwalk

In 1905 the residents of Holly Beach and Wildwood celebrated the connecting of their two boardwalks—now a combined 2½ miles long—at 26th Avenue. The new walkway ran south along the beachfront, terminating at

The Easter parade in front of the old Starlight Ballroom. This venue for vaudeville, big bands, and later rock and roll was also site of the first ABC television broadcast of *Dick Clark's American Bandstand*.

In the early 1930s, the Wildwood walkway recreated a Seminole village, including a show in which tribesmen from the Florida Everglades staged wrestling matches with imported alligators. The World's Champion Pole Sitter, Harry "Had" Elliott, publicized the dramatic contest to people on the boardwalk.

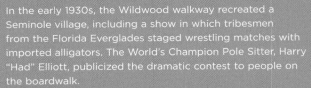

During the Great Depression marathon dancing became an overnight fad and a way for desperate couples to earn a dollar. Almost every ballroom in the country featured the sometimes dangerous activity to keep their doors open during the Depression. Cash prizes were awarded to the couple who could outlast the other contestants, with just a few short breaks provided for food, rest, and other necessities. The demeaning activity could be quite lucrative for the promoters, with some amassing fortunes from the dimes and quarters that the down-and-out public would pay to watch the contestants dance, faint, and in a few cases even die. The first Wildwood dance marathon was won by a couple that danced from June 25 until September 14. The city outlawed the controversial activity in 1931.

Cresse Avenue. To understand the story of the Wildwood boardwalk, one needs to know that sections of the walkway were moved quite often. In 1911 the boardwalk, along with the Casino Pier, was moved closer to the Atlantic. A few years later North Wildwood was forced to take the plunge again and move its 26-foot walkway closer to the sea. As the beach expanded, with new sand building up each year, the boardwalk was farther and farther away from the Atlantic. Photographs of the first walkway show the surf crashing along the pilings under the boards, while later ones show the boardwalk high and dry.

Additional restaurants and bathhouses began to appear along the boardwalk, and by 1906 rolling chairs made their debut. With the boardwalk now spanning more than 2 miles, a ride in the quaint wicker rolling chairs became quite fashionable. The wide beaches were so crowded that in 1907 Sweet's Baths was created. The facility provided 300 changing rooms and hot and cold showers, and, like all bathhouses of the era, towels and swimsuits rented by the hour. It was later lost in a fire in 1923.

The wooden walkway was becoming a wonderful place to do business; more than one million visitors came in 1915. More change came to the island as Holly Beach became part of the city of Wildwood in 1912. Anglesea was renamed North Wildwood in 1910, and Wildwood Crest—or "the Crest"—was founded in 1905. (The Crest would eventually replace its boardwalk with a paved street, so the Wildwood boardwalk of today is located in North Wildwood and Wildwood.)

In 1924, four years after Oliver Bright's midnight raid and his recall as commissioner, the boardwalk faced yet another challenge—an infestation of worms had undermined the stability of its supporting cedar pilings. In addition, the boardwalk needed once again to be relocated closer to the ocean. A petition presented to the city requested the boardwalk be moved from Atlantic Avenue to Beach Avenue. This was no easy task, as the local governments were forever entangled in lawsuits, with merchants and property owners fearful that moving the walkway would impede access to their enterprises or possibly even land-lock their parcel. As a court case concerning the value of the lots where the boardwalk was to be relocated raged on, the wildwood worms continued to feast on their own boardwalk treat, saltwater cedar.

Above: As public taste changed Wildwood's boardwalk promoters searched for new concepts and thrill rides to stay competitive with Atlantic City and Asbury Park. This 1960 aerial view shows some of these changes. The large pier on the right was Hunt's Pier, built on the old site of the Ocean Pier. Its famous roller coaster, the Flyer, designed by the Philadelphia Toboggan Company, opened on Memorial Day 1957 and was an immediate success. The Sportland Pier can be seen farther up the beach.

Below: Another view of Hunt's Pier, the famous Flyer roller coaster, and the Wildwood Sightseer Tram. The pier was the number one attraction on the boardwalk when this photograph was taken.

The worms were victorious, and the city was forced to demolish the walk from 26th to Oak Avenues and replace the damaged wooden pilings with reinforced concrete. The new Wildwood boardwalk was completed, and a parade was held in celebration on Memorial Day of 1925. By 1927 a new walkway was completed from Montgomery to Cresse Avenues. With the construction

THE WILDWOOD BABY PARADE

The first Wildwood Baby Parade was born in 1909 and awarded prizes in numerous categories. If your baby was not the prettiest, there was always the chance junior could take home the prize for the best dressed—or even the fattest baby. Prizes ranged from cash to taffy and fudge donated by local merchants. (One hopes the fattest baby received currency as a prize.) The parade grew in popularity, and in 1936 the *New York Times* reported that 100,000 spectators witnessed the event as that year's "Queen Oceania" reviewed the children on parade from her royal boardwalk throne. Two years earlier a new category, pets, was added to the annual event. Categories today include most attractive baby boy and girl, fancy children riding (strollers, coaches, kiddie cars, and wagons), comic or most original children riding, fancy dress walking, and comic-original dress walking. The fattest baby category has gone the way of the 5-cent cigar.

of a new North Wildwood boardwalk in 1928 at a cost of $400,000, the Wildwood boardwalk as we know it today was in place. It begins in the southern end at Cresse Avenue and runs approximately 2 miles to North Wildwood. Most "board rats" are so preoccupied with their funnel cakes and next amusement ride as they walk the boards that they do not notice that the walks do not line up at 26th Avenue, where the North Wildwood boardwalk wed the Wildwood walkway. There is also a slight curve where the Wildwood boardwalk met the old Holly Beach boardwalk at Cedar Avenue.

From the time the first plank was placed on the beach, with a series of disjointed boardwalks adjoining the Five-Mile Beach communities, to the late 1920s, when a unified boardwalk was in place, the promoters had to find new and interesting ways to keep the crowds coming. As Wildwood grew in popularity, its two major competitors became clear: Asbury Park and Atlantic City. Statistics for the major summer holidays by 1930 showed Wildwood surpassing Ocean City and Cape May, but running a distant third to the big two resorts to the north. The Five-Mile Beach communities realized that a well-maintained, well-policed wooden walkway packed with amusements, food concessions, theaters, and bathhouses was the key to success, and they supported the majority of the enterprises.

As the crowds increased, the piers expanded to accommodate them. The Crest Pier in Wildwood Crest was destroyed by a fire in 1919 and replaced with a new facility. Although new piers would appear from time to time, Ocean Pier continued to reign supreme. When it was sold in 1921, the new owners began investing heavily to upgrade the ballroom and skating rink and to add rides.

In 1928 competition arrived in the form of Sportland, built on the North Wildwood walkway between 23rd and 24th Avenues and offering a massive pool, tennis courts, volleyball courts, basketball courts, and a variety of sports-related activities. Unfortunately for the owners, the new venture opened just before the stock market crash of 1929 and a worldwide depression that pushed most amusement facilities either onto the brink or over the edge. The same period saw the foreclosure of Edward Rhoads's Amusement Park, along with his now-famous Jack Rabbit wooden roller coaster. The new owners, the Cedar-Schellenger Corporation, took advantage of their riparian rights to expand the amusement park into a pier, called Marine Pier. The inland section, complete with the Jack Rabbit, became known as Playland, with a new, brightly lit arched entrance.

The Great Depression ruined financially weak promoters and provided bargains and opportunities for those with deep pockets. As an example, movie theater mogul William C. Hunt purchased the failing Ocean Pier in 1935 for only $200,000. He then went about restoring it to a first-class pier, borrowing heavily from Coney Island's George Tilyou and hiring Tilyou's former Steeplechase Park manager. (Tilyou's Steeplechase Park featured attractions that not only provided laughs but also challenged the Victorian values of decorum and separation of the sexes. He was the first to create the

Then as now, the more unusual the attraction the better. This photograph depicts the Swooper, a popular ride at Playland in the 1930s.

The Jumbo Jet was purchased by Bill and Will Morey at the Oktoberfest in Europe and installed in Wildwood in 1976. This 56-foot-high roller coaster by the premier steel-track coaster designer in the world established the Morey brothers in the amusement business.

Human Roulette Wheel, where men and women would ride a spinning, horizontal wheel as it traveled faster and faster, eventually depositing the riders in a very daring pile of humanity—this during a time when a woman required an escort to travel to the seashore.) The Ocean Pier Funchase gave adventure seekers an array of daring rides, including the sliding floor (guaranteed to provide a quick introduction to the man or woman sliding next to you), the rocking staircase, and a gargantuan slide. Hunt also added new theaters, a carousel, a circus rink, and a roller coaster, the Whirlwind. Ever the promoter, Hunt booked the most fashionable bands of the day at his Ocean Pier Starlight Ballroom, and he seemed to have the Midas touch.

Not unlike the twists, turns, and sudden drops of a roller coaster, fate seems to always have something unpredictable in mind for the Wildwood boardwalk. On Christmas Day 1943, a horrific fire claimed the magical Ocean Pier along with Sagel's Saltwater Taffy, several apartments, and scores of other businesses. This was at the height of World War II, when the Jersey coastline was subject to blackouts out of concern for Nazi submarine attacks. A rumor floated through town of an explosion heard offshore just before the fire—perhaps a German submarine shelling the Ocean Pier—but this was never substantiated.

After the war millions of soldiers returned home to join their families and rebuild their lives. America welcomed back its heroes, and as the 1950s approached, the country entered an unprecedented era of prosperity. For Wildwood and other Jersey Shore points, this represented a major opportunity, as change came in many forms. The railroads merged and cut services for good as Americans chose the automobile as their preferred means of travel. Hotels suffered as motels began appearing around the country, a change still apparent. Wildwood is to 1950s motel architecture what Cape May is to Victorian architecture. Love them or hate them, motels were here to stay.

Transportation on the Wildwood boardwalk also changed as the famous trams made their appearance in 1949, replacing the old roller chairs. Conventions became a major source of revenue for the shore resorts, and Wildwood competed with Asbury Park and Atlantic City for the more lucrative gatherings. In 1957 the Hunt

organization reentered the pier business with Hunt's Pier, the major draw being the Flyer roller coaster built by the Philadelphia Toboggan Company. The Hunt family invested heavily to provide 1950s tourists with new and exciting attractions, including Panther sports cars, a Scrambler, and an array of children's rides. They later added Oceanic Wonderland, with the Satellite and a ride called Crazy Dazy. In 1959 came Jungleland, a Disney-style passenger ride that toured an animated "jungle" complete with rhinos, crocodiles, monkeys, and even human inhabitants. In the late 1950s, Hunt's Starlight Ballroom was the venue for pioneer rock stars and the location of historic radio and television broadcasts of

hops by a then-newcomer on the scene, Dick Clark.

Casino Arcade, owned and operated by the Ramagosa family, was by then a nationally renowned Kiddieland. Impressed with the Hunts' success, they expanded with an array of exciting rides that included a local favorite, the Bubble Bounce. In the style of all old-school board-walk showmen, the Ramagosa family even added a replica of a Florida Seminole village with a daily wrestling match, man versus alligator. The Ramagosas also owned Sportland, which hosted thrilling, daredevil attractions such as the Human Comet, who would cover himself with gasoline and jump from a platform into a flaming water tank. Gentler children's amusements were added

Above: Today Morey's Piers offers more than just rides. Also available is a cornucopia of boardwalk foods, from Curley's Fries and Funnel Cakes to Dippin Dots and waffles and ice cream. Morey's brochure says it all: "Get Very Wet, Scream, Laugh and Indulge."

Right: A vintage view of the Wildwood walkway. The Ed Rhoads Amusement Park carousel building can be seen on the left, just behind the Western Union Telegraph sign.

for the weaker at heart. A new pier, Fun Pier, also made its debut during the 1950s. Promoter Joe Barnes built this new amusement destination by rehabilitating an old, dilapidated pier that had been the location for one of the city's first convention centers. Fun Pier featured a Sky Ride and several other theme park–style attractions.

Another major boom for the entire Jersey Shore came with the completion of the Garden State Parkway in 1955. It became the highway that residents love to hate, as its mythical summer traffic jams caused by numerous tollbooths also meant a steady stream of visitors to Wildwood and competing shore points. The boardwalk continued to prosper, and by 1960 five major amusement facilities lined the walkway. The Hunts continued to invest to keep their rides and amusements current with the public tastes. Inexpensive air travel now provided new opportunities, and it was essential to find ways to keep the crowds coming. In response, the Hunts built the eight-car Golden Nugget Mine Ride, and later added the Skua, a pirate ship funhouse.

The Fun Pier now began to provide the Hunts with serious competition, with a variety of state-of-the-art rides and attractions. Marine Pier also expanded, along with Casino Arcade and Sportland. Things were looking up

for Wildwood, and by the 1960s the town ranked just behind Asbury Park and Atlantic City for the lucrative convention trade.

In the 1970s Wildwood operated six amusement piers: Hunt's, Fun Pier, Sportland, Surfside Pier, Marine Pier, and Casino Arcade. That would soon change, for this decade marked a period of monumental decline for the entire Jersey Shore. Pollution; competition from Disney, Las Vegas, and other resorts; inexpensive jet travel; and an increase in crime were just some of the reasons why business declined. Age-old competitors of Wildwood traveled in a variety of new directions. Asbury Park spiraled into urban blight and is only today on the road to recovery. Atlantic City, with the blessing of the state of New Jersey, turned to legalized gambling. Cape May realized its future was its past and is now a National Historic Landmark city.

Neglect also helped dim the lights of the old walkways. In the early 1970s the Wildwood boardwalk was in need of repairs that the city claimed it could not afford. The city received a handout of sorts when New Jersey senator Harrison Williams arranged to have the lumber used to construct the presidential reviewing stands and seating for the 1973 inaugural parade to be sold to the ailing

When the boardwalk was moved, a key building was often moved along with it. In an era when labor was less expensive than lumber, skilled crews could take all the time needed to carefully transport a building. Pictured here is the Ocean Pier being moved along with the boardwalk closer to the Atlantic Ocean.

The Ed Rhoads Amusement Park also included in 1919 a carousel custom built by the Philadelphia Toboggan Company and the extremely popular Ye Old Mill, an early-twentieth-century version of a tunnel of love. Pictured is the entrance to the Jack Rabbit and Ye Old Mill.

resort to rebuild parts of its boardwalk. The $400,000 worth of lumber was bought for $150,000, including transportation from the capital. Wildwood's city commissioner, Wilbur Ostrander, told the *New York Times*, "It includes everything but the Presidential seal and the bullet-proof glass." He added that the lumber would be enough to redeck the walkway twice over. The lumber was from President Richard Nixon's second inauguration. Just four years later Wildwood again benefited from a presidential inauguration and purchased more lumber (only the press-box wood this time) from President Jimmy Carter's big day. Apparently, the city was a nonpartisan bargain hunter.

By the late 1980s a Wildwood tradition, the Annual Baby Parade, came to an end due to lack of interest (it is back in business today). The piers were the glue that was barely holding the ailing resort together, and as the old operators retired, sold off, or died, the future of the Jersey Shore's most exciting amusement walkway was in peril. There was an opportunity to once again prosper because Atlantic City, once the undisputed king of the boardwalk pier, had turned its back on amusement piers for a roll of the dice.

When the Hunt family sold its pier in 1985, the new owners were unwilling or unable to restore it to its former glory. Its landmark coaster, the Flyer, was razed in 1989 in order for the pier to expand. (The Jack Rabbit coaster had been razed five years earlier.) In 1996 fate smiled when the Catanoso family won almost $10 million in the New Jersey State Lottery and bought the aging pier. They loved the business and invested their lottery windfall (along with some of their bank's money) to modernize the old Hunt's Pier, renamed Dinosaur Beach Adventure.

Gilbert Ramagosa had inherited Casino Arcade and Sportland in the 1970s, and operated a successful operation along with a diversified portfolio of other business interests. In 1964 a fire had destroyed the Casino Arcade's new Mars Ride, and sadly, three children lost their lives in the blaze. He paved over the area as a parking lot, and local historians feel the tragedy took the heart out of the amusement business for him. In the mid-1980s Ramagosa sold Sportland and the Casino Arcade property, and a decade later sold his boardwalk tram business.

An earlier boardwalk move caused the popular Casino to become landlocked, so in 1911 the Casino Arcade, pictured here, was built to permit access to the Casino from the beach and new boardwalk.

The Wildwood Renaissance

It became apparent to Wildwood watchers and the loyal fans of the aging resort that the famous boardwalk was in desperate need of a knight in shining armor. Luckily, two appeared, brothers Bill and Will Morey. They were no strangers to the resort. Will owned a construction business and was involved in Wildwood's building expansion during the boom era. A skilled carpenter, he was also directly involved in building many of the 1950s-era Doo Wop–style motels that make Wildwood so unique today. His brother Bill had been active in several successful concessions on the Wildwood walkway.

As chance would have it, the two were vacationing in Florida in 1968 when a roadside amusement attraction caught their eye. As they studied the sleek, twelve-lane, fiberglass waterslide, the brothers knew that they were looking at Wildwood's future. Now all they needed was a

spot to build one of these contraptions along the Jersey Shore. Back in New Jersey, the brothers purchased a miniature-golf complex and small restaurant on the boardwalk that had fallen on hard times. These were on two small piers separated by a small slice of land owned by the city. To make things worse, the city also owned the boardwalk frontage and only permitted the pier owners access via a narrow walkway. Although the location was hardly the ideal, it was all they could afford. They installed their waterslide, named Wipe Out, over the miniature-golf pier and leased the space on their other pier to help cash flow. They proudly named their new venture Surfside Pier, and as they say, the rest is history.

Although not an overnight success, the Moreys were rather the living embodiment of the old phrase "The harder I work, the luckier I get." Their combination of boardwalk concession and construction knowledge mixed well with their instinct on what was the "next big thing" in amusements. When an opportunity knocked, they took advantage, but never acted recklessly. An example is the Marine Pier/Casino Arcade complex. When it was put on the market, the owner decided wisely to sell the properties as two separate parcels because of the high price tag, and while the Moreys would have loved to own both, they settled on only one because it was within their budget.

Things did not always run smoothly, as when the land came on the market that separated their two piers at Surfside Pier. They became engaged in a protracted legal battle with the city and competitors but were eventually able to acquire the parcel to unify their property and create Morey's Pier. Here the brothers provided unique attractions, often traveling to Europe to discover the next generation of thrill rides. One such trip in 1976 led to the purchase of Jumbo Jet, a 56-foot-high roller coaster designed by the premier steel-track coaster designer in the world. This state-of-the-art ride put the Moreys on the amusement map in this country.

As the years passed, they acquired competing piers, including the old Marine Pier, which they renovated and reopened as Mariner's Landing in 1977 with three European rides. They acquired the old Fun Deck Pier in 1987. If a ride became outdated, they often sold it off in search of the next thrill machine. Their sons joined the organization, and Morey's was the quintessential family-owned and -operated business.

In 1995 they installed a signature ride, the Great Nor'easter, a monstrous, steel-railed roller coaster. Another gargantuan ride, the Great White roller coaster, the first major wooden roller coaster to be built in Wildwood since the 1919 Jack Rabbit, was installed in 1996.

Today Morey's is synonymous with the Wildwood boardwalk. They currently operate Morey's Piers, located at 25th Avenue, which offers over thirty rides, including the Great Nor'easter roller coaster. On the old Hunt's Pier they currently operate two go-kart tracks. Morey's Piers, located at Schellenger Avenue, offers thirty rides, including a Ferris wheel, the Sky Cycle monorail, and another roller coaster. Then there's Morey's Piers at Spencer Avenue, where the Great White roller coaster and fifteen other attractions reside. While it would be unfair to credit the Morey family alone for the Wildwood boardwalk renaissance, without a doubt they put the "wild" back in Wildwood.

The Wildwoods now boast a brand-new 260,000-square-foot Convention Center on the boardwalk—an indication of the state and business community's confidence in the resort. Additionally, an organization called the Doo Wop Preservation League is working to preserve motels and other structures representing the unique 1950s style of architecture. Their dream is to have Doo Wop do for Wildwood what Victoriana has done for Cape May. Some residents question the viability of such a plan, as many buildings have already fallen victim to the wrecking ball and the owners of the remaining 1950s-era motels are courted daily by condominium developers with fat checkbooks.

What cannot be doubted is that the Wildwood boardwalk is the best remaining example of the classic Jersey Shore wooden walkway. Though it may not be for everyone, a stroll on this boardwalk on a hot summer night is the real experience. The shrill voices of the game barkers, the screams of the thrill riders, the disembodied "watch the tram" voice, and the competing music from hundreds of rides and concessions blend with a thousand turning gears and the laughs of ten thousand families to create a cacophony of pure Jersey boardwalk. More than 70,000 wooden planks stretch for nearly 2 miles jam-packed with amusement piers, food vendors, and games of chance.

Unlike most of the Jersey Shore, Wildwood's wide, ever-growing beach is still free, with no beach tags required. As the beach expands each year, the amusement piers have more free available land to grow their businesses—and the walkway itself is farther and farther away from the ocean. If you ask most people in Cape May or Atlantic City where their beach went, they will point to Wildwood. The truth is that Wildwood beach has filled in from both the north and the south, thanks to an ill-thought plan where jetties were constructed at the Cape May inlet by the Army Corps of Engineers many years ago. Wildwood has sections of its strand where it could actually fit another city block. Because of that, it is the only New Jersey barrier island where dune or beach replenishments have ever been required.

Who knows, perhaps a midnight raid similar to the Oliver Bright hatchet party of 1920 may be in the future. Until then, the happy board rats with hot dogs, curly fries, funnel cakes, and Italian ice in hand will have to don their flip-flops and make the ¼-mile walk through the white, hot sand from the boardwalk to the surf, loving every minute of it.

Cape May

Cape May in 1868 was the first New Jersey resort to construct a boardwalk, or "flirtation walk." As one newspaper reported, "Leading along the beach over one thousand feet…is a wide plank walk, which will prove very agreeable to all who do not desire to walk on the sand."

A wonderful view of the Cape May boardwalk and a couple stopping to chat with some friends in a horseless carriage. The famous ornamental arches, each one lit with a series of electric bulbs, can be seen along the boardwalk. The building in the center right is Denizot's Ocean View Cottage on Beach Drive, constructed after the devastating fire of 1878. On the far right are the pillars of the original Lafayette Hotel demolished in 1970.

In August 1847 the traditional "season" at Cape May was winding down. The wealthy families that summered at the tony resort were closing their cottages and departing in droves to begin the autumn social season in Philadelphia, Baltimore, New York City, or Washington, D.C. Hotel guests were also returning home, and, in turn, the major hostelries sent their house orchestras along with much of the staff packing for the winter. All was peaceful in the city that—along with Newport, Rhode Island, and Saratoga Springs, New York—was a favorite of America's movers and shakers.

Then news arrived that a genuine nineteenth-century superstar was about to pay the Summer City by the Sea an unexpected visit. Henry Clay, the most prominent congressional leader of the era and perhaps the most formidable politician ever to have served in Washington, had suffered a terrible personal loss with the death of his son in the Mexican War. Clay told the press, "Finding myself in a theatre of sadness, I thought I would fly to the mountain top and descend to the waves of the ocean, and my meeting with the sympathy of friends, obtain relief to the sadness which encompassed me." In choosing Cape May for his retreat, he was to add significantly to its national prominence among resorts.

A unique Cape May boardwalk memory is of the summer railroad station, seen on the right of this image. It was located opposite the boardwalk on Grant Street. Built in 1876 by the West Jersey Railroad at a cost of $20,000, it transported eager tourists right up to the boardwalk and beach during the summer season. The railroad's Sea Breeze Excursion House was located next to the station.

Although Clay had unsuccessfully run for the presidency of the United States five times, his intellectual prowess—and more importantly, his steely integrity—had made him a national celebrity. In 1833 he had become the leader of the newly created Whig Party. His efforts in settling disputes over the slavery issue and keeping the North and South united for many years prior to the Civil War had earned him the epithet "the Great Compromiser."

Henry Clay's plan for an off-season vacation in Cape May was about as successful as his presidential campaigns. The hotels began to overflow with guests as if it were July, with the owners frantically reaching out to the locals to fill the positions of staff who had returned home. To the delight of hotel owner Richard Smith Ludlam, Clay chose his hotel, the Mansion House, for himself and his family. The house band had already departed for the season, so Ludlam arranged to have an orchestra travel with the Clay entourage on the steamboat from Philadelphia to Cape May.

Hundreds of nineteenth-century "groupies" swarmed the tiny resort from all points to get a look at the Great Compromiser. Even dignitaries joined the frenzy, including the newspaper tycoon Horace Greeley, who hired a special steamboat to take his group direct from

The eastern terminus of the Cape May boardwalk at Sewell's Point circa 1900. The Cape May, Delaware Bay, and Sewell's Point Railroad began transporting tourists with horse-drawn trolleys that ran along the beachfront from the steamship wharf at Cape May Point to the popular Inlet House hotel

on Sewell's Point, located at the eastern end of Cape May. The trolleys were later converted to steam and eventually to electricity. During the summer season, trolleys were operated as open-air cars.

New York City to Cape May. Envoys from every major city were dispatched to entice the famous legislator to change his plans and travel with them back to their metropolis. Such was the value of the Henry Clay "brand." The celebrity guest did not disappoint. He held the crowds spellbound as he gave a speech in the Kersal, the Mansion House's pavilion and ballroom, built at the beginning of the season. He took a sea bath twice daily, and on each occasion he was mobbed by frantic female admirers, scissors in hand, attempting to shear a lock of his hair for a souvenir (hair wreaths being extremely popular in this era). Clay and his family stayed at the resort for almost two weeks, and to no one's surprise, the newspapers reported that his hair was noticeably shorter when he returned to Washington, D.C.

Queen of the Seaside Resorts

While the Henry Clay visit helped fill hotels for the following season, Cape May had by the mid-nineteenth century already earned the title Queen of the Seaside Resorts. Although Long Branch residents may disagree, most historians regard Cape May as the first seaside resort on the Jersey Shore. The reason? Location, location, location. By 1790 Philadelphia had one of the busiest seaports in North America, and fleets of ships and boats would daily make the voyage down the Delaware River, round Cape May (New Jersey's southernmost tip), and head for New York, Boston, and other major seaports. In an era of primitive roads and no railroads, it didn't take long for some enterprising sea captain to realize that he could pick up a few dollars dropping passengers off at Cape May to spend a few weeks on the beautiful Jersey Shore.

Next in line was another enterprising group—local farmers and fishermen who saw the opportunity to rent a room or two to vacationers in need of shelter. Later came the hotels and boardinghouses, and an industry was born on the New Jersey coast. As early as 1766 an advertisement in the *Pennsylvania Gazette* for a plantation to be sold in Cape May noted the 254 acres of land were "within One Mile and a Half of the Sea Shore; where a Number resort for Health, and bathing in the Water." Health was the draw for fashionable families wealthy enough to escape the heat of overcrowded, disease-ridden colonial cities who learned from the London newspapers that King George III had taken up sea bathing for his health.

Cape May's exponential growth throughout the nineteenth century was fueled by Philadelphia's expansion.

Above: Shade tents were emblematic of the Cape May beach. In the background stretches the Iron Pier. Built in 1884, it replaced the Victor Denizot amusement pier that was lost to a fire in 1878. The new pier was a major attraction in Cape May, with a theater at the ocean end offering light opera and, later, vaudeville. The pier contained more than a half-acre of floor space and provided summer revelers with an 8,000-square-foot dance floor where festive hops were held weekly. Popular bands of the day also gave daily concerts during the summer season.

Below: The entrance of the Iron Pier provided retail space for merchants of unusual items that were popular along the shore during the late nineteenth century. This circa 1900 photo shows visitors shopping for their souvenirs from Chong, Hop, Hing and Company, and Schwartz's Bazaar.

Larger and more fashionable hotels replaced the great white barn-like structures that originally housed the thousands of sojourners who migrated to the popular watering hole each season from July 1 to September 1. More celebrities followed in Henry Clay's footsteps, including presidents of the United States. (Contrary to local folklore, Abraham Lincoln was not one of them. A Mansion House ledger does indicate an A. Lincoln and wife visiting the hotel on July 31, 1849—but the future president of the United States was a thousand miles away that day, filing an affidavit for a client in Illinois. During the time the ledger was signed, a grocer by the name of Abel Lincoln resided in Philadelphia. As I noted in a previous publication, The Summer City by the Sea: Cape May, New Jersey (1998), I believe that many Cape May residents and authors are confusing the Great Emancipator with the green grocer.

Button's Blank Canvas

Like other resorts, Cape May experienced the ebbs and flows dictated by weather, fire, war, economic factors, and just plain fashion. It was popular with southerners because of its proximity to Baltimore and Washington, D.C. The Mason-Dixon Line that was only supposed to establish the Maryland–Pennsylvania border became emblematic as the dividing line between the North and South. Extending that line eastward, a sizable section of the Jersey Shore falls below the Mason-Dixon Line.

The Civil War sent a good many southerners packing from Cape May, and most summered elsewhere after the war ended. Yet each time the city seemed to be dealt a fatal blow, something would occur to bounce it back. The post–Civil War growth of the railroads brought easy access to Cape May, creating a robust cottage boom as families could now own a cottage and commute on weekends via the railroad. By the late 1870s Cape May's popularity had waned a bit. It was no longer considered a major competitor of Newport, Rhode Island, where "summer cottages" such as the Breakers and Marble House were grander than Cape May's finest hotels. The Summer City by the Sea also lost a portion of its clientele to an upstart resort, Atlantic City, a city created by railroad men and land speculators who shrewdly drew a straight line from Philadelphia to the Atlantic Ocean and built a railroad that created the concept of a day at the beach.

The eastern end of the boardwalk was a desolate place when the Hotel Cape May was under construction in the winter of 1906. Today the entire area is filled with beautiful cottages. The hotel was razed in 1996, and the land was subdivided into seaside lots that were sold to assist in the financing of the restoration of Congress Hall.

Just six years after the completion of the hotel, the area to its east is no longer isolated or barren.

Fire constantly threatened the existence of wooden cities by the sea, and in 1878 a great conflagration destroyed thirty-five acres in the heart of Cape May. Arson was believed to be the cause; and as the fire took place in November, the hotels were empty, and there was miraculously no loss of life. The year before the fire a passenger on a sailboat described the impressive Cape May skyline on a clear summer evening, "flashing lines of festival lights connecting the continuous row of monstrous four-floored buildings, seeming to touch each other...." That was all lost. But the resort was popular enough and its real estate so highly valued that the city immediately began to rebuild. Once the rubble of the fire was cleared, the property owners of Cape May were presented with a thirty-five acre tract and a decision. Should they build wooden giants in an effort to compete with Atlantic City and other larger resorts, or should they limit the town's growth and build on a more intimate scale? They chose the latter—a decision that would eventually create the National Historical Landmark city that is so highly prized today.

For example, instead of rebuilding the massive Congress Hall hotel, the northern end of the hotel footprint was subdivided; a new street, Congress Place, was cut through the property, and cottage lots were sold. Congress Hall was rebuilt as a smaller version of the grand hotel it had been at the time of the fire, using brick to assure the public that it was now fireproof. Its traditional L-shaped style provided an ocean view for the maximum number of rooms.

By 1878 aging architect Stephen Decatur Button, fashionable before the Civil War, had been pushed aside for more trendy designers like Vanderbilt favorite Richard Morris Hunt. The Cape May fire represented an opportunity for Button to make one final mark, and he did so with the energy of a twenty-year-old. He not only directly or indirectly designed several significant projects, but his affinity for the simply ornamented Italianate style influenced the reconstruction in another way. The majority of postfire cottages were built without architectural plans, the local builders either following the lines of existing Button cottages or borrowing

Above: Cape May's Convention Hall and pier were constructed in 1916 and became the place for most of the significant social events of each summer. Katherine Vonahnen, who spent most of her life in Cape May, recalls "concerts and lectures, fashion shows and flower exhibits, ballroom dancing, and the annual crowning of Queen Maysea who was chosen from those participants in the Baby Parade." She fondly remembers the "Kiddie Revue" that was held every Friday evening during the summer season. "I was born showing off . . . being the first girl born in my father's family for 122 years" she notes, "REALLY!!!"

Below: A late 1950s view of the Cape May boardwalk and Convention Hall complex a few years before the Great Atlantic Storm of 1962 destroyed the entire beach-front. Notice how the boardwalk curves seaward where it meets Convention Hall. When the old trolley ran along the boardwalk, it crossed from the beach onto Beach Drive at that point and then crossed back to the ocean side of the walkway after it passed the historic structure.

The Baby Parade along the boardwalk in the early 1930s.
Who would be this year's Queen Maysea? Convention Hall
and Pier can be seen in the background.

Above: The city provided a series of pavilions along the beach at the end of the nineteenth century. Until Convention Hall was built in 1916, residents and tourists used the small boardwalk structures for concerts and other civic events. This pavilion located on the walkway at Beach Drive and Grant Street was still active in the early 1940s.

Below: The Solarium, located on the boardwalk alongside Convention Hall, was a favorite place for beach lovers to take a break from the noonday sun. An information booth was conveniently located inside the pavilion. Today a clone of the historic building now stands on the promenade.

plans from the popular pattern books of the era. The city that so many people have come to love today, with its more than six hundred examples of Victorian architecture and its intimate scale, can thank architect-artist Stephen Decatur Button and the unknown arsonist who unwittingly presented Button with his thirty-five-acre blank canvas.

"Flirtation Walk"

Throughout most of its long history as a resort, Cape May has been blessed with the best strand on the East Coast, its gentle-sloping beachfront floor of beautiful white sand the envy of its competitors. This famous strand also drove the fast-paced reconstruction after the 1878 fire. The city quickly repaired the boardwalk, extending it from Broadway to Madison Avenue and, by 1880, illuminating it with gas lamps purchased from the Pennsylvania Globe Gas Light Company. The lights were placed at equal distances, seventy paces, along the entire length of the boardwalk.

Records indicate that Cape May was the first New Jersey resort to construct a boardwalk, or "flirtation walk," as it was known in the late 1860s. In July 1868, two years before Atlantic City's walkway was constructed, the *Ocean Wave* newspaper reported on the Cape May boardwalk, noting, "Leading along the beach over one thousand feet to the other hotels is a wide plank walk, which will prove very agreeable to all who do not desire to walk on the sand."

Boardwalks tend to reflect the character of their city, and in the case of Cape May, the walkway never possessed a carnival or boisterous atmosphere. Like many walkways of wood, the Cape May boardwalk had a series of piers. As the value of seaside real estate increased, it did not take long for a savvy businessperson to realize that for the price of a boardwalk lot, he could extend his "land" out to sea via a pier. In Cape May this individual was Victor Denizot, a wealthy cottage owner, who built a wooden pier opposite the Hotel Lafayette. The original Congress Hall hotel also constructed a pier. The fire of 1878 destroyed Denizot's pier—just weeks after an 80-mile-an-hour gale took out a large section of the Congress Hall pier.

The Denizot Pier, rebuilt in 1884 as the Cape May Iron Pier, would remain a popular boardwalk location until abandoned and razed in 1910—a victim of erosion,

Everyone was expected to dress in their Sunday finest when walking the boards. Pictured are two such boardwalk strollers, who are clearly enjoying the day.

Above: Poet Katherine Vonahnen, now in her eighties, grew up in Cape May. In this image from a bygone era, she is the little girl on the left with the pails and shovels. Her little brother is seated in the front of the pyramid, her father is in the bottom center, and her mother on top of him in the next row. Old Convention Hall and the fishing pier can be seen in the background.

Below: Bathhouses were a necessity in an era when, as Katherine Vonahnen's recalls, " a lady would never be seen in her bathing suit on the street or in any public place." Ms. Vonahnen remembers how her grandmother would take her to the Cape May beach where they would change into their suits in Maguire's bathhouses, pictured here with some dandies sitting in front. In the background are several of the famous "Seven Sisters," or Atlantic Terrace cottages. The identical homes were designed by Stephen Decatur Button and built in 1891-92.

storms, accidents, and eventually fire. When it was first built, the pier had a charming little theater on the ocean end, where noted opera artists of the era performed (it was later changed to a vaudeville venue). As was the custom of the day, the pier had several "exotic" shops at its entrance, including Chong, Hop, Hing and Company, retailers of fine Chinese and Japanese goods, and Schwartz's Bazaar, specializing in Mexican goods.

In July 1896 a new boardwalk was built, 16 feet wide and extending the entire length of the beachfront. A railing lined the ocean side of the walkway, which also had city-installed benches for strollers. By the turn of the century, the resort also had a city pier and boasted a series of distinct arches that were used to illuminate the boardwalk. Mock trials were a fad of the day, and in 1895 local newspapers reported that the mayor was "tried" for introducing electric lights along the boardwalk and "spoiling the girls' spooning." In addition, a delightful electric trolley ran the entire length of the beach from the eastern end at Sewell's Point all the way west to Cape May Point. During the summer season, the trolley ran open-air cars. Another popular beachfront amusement at the time was automobile racing on the hard, flat Cape May strand. In 1905 the public was treated to Henry Ford's racing his six-cylinder "Wonder" against a field of world-renowned drivers. One year later the *New York Times* reported that the city had extended its boardwalk to 5 miles in length, and that rolling chairs would be next. In 1913 the Sewell's Point Amusement Palace opened, along with the Madison Avenue Theatre and the Marine Casino at Howard Street and Beach Drive.

Changing Times

As the century progressed, the boardwalk evolved, and a need was recognized for a Convention Hall and new pier. Completed in 1916, the convention building quickly became a center for the city's social activities. Its handsome pier extended from the boardwalk over the rolling surf, providing a wonderful promenade and fishing pier, complete with a big blue pennant with CONVENTION HALL FISHING PIER embroidered on it. The hall structure provided retail space, a theater, and meeting rooms for the Boy Scouts, American Legion, and Chamber of Commerce. The ballroom supplied space for 600 couples to dance to orchestra music, provided nightly during the busy summer season. Special concerts with noted orchestras were also held each Sunday night during the season. The building offered a public solarium

The large, wooden Cape May walkway in the late 1940s. After the 1962 storm, a macadam promenade replaced the venerable planked walk.

Today the Cape May boardwalk is in effect a wide seawall, affectionately referred to by the locals as the "promenade."

on its south side, in addition to a series of numbered pavilions along the boardwalk.

Storms remained a constant threat to the walkway, and on February 7, 1920, an unnamed hurricane destroyed the boardwalk and damaged Convention Hall, the fishing pier, and Pavilion #1. It was the worst storm to hit Cape May in fifty years. Undaunted, the city commissioners vowed to rebuild that spring, and by the summer the resort was back in business.

The Great Atlantic Hurricane of 1944 severely damaged the walkway and all associated buildings, along with most of the eastern seaboard. The city rebuilt the boardwalk in record time, despite the material and labor shortages created by World War II. In 1962 the Great Atlantic Storm, the worst storm to hit Cape May in recorded history, destroyed all but two blocks of the boardwalk, along with Convention Hall. Hunt's Pier, a Cape May landmark since 1920, was one of the first victims of the powerful northeaster. The mechanical games that had provided joy for generations of children became destructive missiles as they were hurled across Beach Avenue, wreaking havoc on the historic hotels that lined the drive. This time the city, working with state and federal grants, constructed a scaled-down ver-

sion of Convention Hall, along with a macadam seawall "promenade" to replace the boardwalk and provide protection against the next "big one."

Cape May's Treasures

Today Cape May's storybook renaissance has made it the gold standard of resorts. Cape May joined an elite club in 1976, when the entire city was designated a National Historic Landmark. A well-managed, dedicated cultural group, the Mid-Atlantic Center for the Arts, or MAC, has successfully lengthened the tourist season by conducting walking and trolley tours and programs, such as the extremely popular Victorian Week in October. Preservationists had finally convinced residents that there was gold in those old Victorian structures, and even the city government realized that the major tourist attraction was not the promenade or even the beach, but the beautiful restored collection of Victorian-era structures throughout the town. Bulldozer planning came to a screeching halt—as witnessed in other resorts along the New Jersey coastline, thoughtless development could damage a city more than hurricane or fire. The robust Cape May Historic Preservation Commission has been charged with assisting residents and working with them

LIGHT OF ASIA

There were no gargantuan Ferris wheels, roller coasters, or carousels on the Cape May boardwalk, although one bigger-than-life attraction began to take shape on the beachfront meadows of South Cape May in 1884. Crowds gathered daily to watch the construction of Light of Asia, a giant wooden elephant that was related to Coney Island's Elephant Hotel or Elephantine Colossus (1882) and Atlantic City's Lucy (1881, now in Margate).The sponsor of Cape May's timber pachyderm was Theodore M. Reger, a land speculator and entrepreneur. He hired Philadelphia architect N. H. Culver to design the beast along the lines of the two older wooden elephants, designed by James V. Lafferty. Reger immediately placed an ad in local newspapers soliciting tenants for the Light of Asia. "Parties wishing rooms in the elephant to sell soda water, fancy articles, advertising, etc, and privilege for bathhouses, ice cream garden and dairy. Apply on premises . . ."

The Light of Asia, or Old Dumbo, as the locals would refer to it, was more than 40 feet tall with a covered pavilion, or "howdah," resting on his back. Both hind legs were equipped with spiral stairs inside, while another set of stairs led to the howdah, allowing Reger to charge 10 cents for the scenic view of the Atlantic Ocean and surrounding meadows. It is estimated that more than one million pieces of wood were required to construct the elephant and 13,000 square feet of tin were used for its "skin." The cost was estimated to be over $18,000 in 1884 dollars, and that would require selling a good deal of ice cream, soda water, fancy articles, and 10-cent howdah tours during the short summer season.

Another difficulty was location. The trolley ran by the beast several times an hour during the summer, but the lighthouse at Cape May Point, also on the trolley route, provided a more impressive view for free.

In the end the Light of Asia was not a financial success, and Reger and his associates used it to promote the development of the Mount Vernon Tract that eventually became the borough of South Cape May. The elephant that stood as a silent sentinel along the Atlantic for almost twenty years was eventually abandoned, fell into disrepair, and became a gathering place for vagrants. It became a hazard to public safety and was razed by the city at the turn of the century.

to ensure that the city's treasures remain intact. Traffic problems are now the issue, and the city may eventually ban nonresidential traffic during the summer season and create an off-site jitney service to ferry tourists to their hotels and bed-and-breakfasts.

In the end, Cape May seems to have won the battle with its major rivals. The mansions of Newport survive today only as museums, and they owe their existence to the Preservation Society of Newport County. Atlantic City has hitched its star to legalized gambling, and Long Branch is in the midst of a controversial redevelopment plan. Cape May has become nationally known and for now seems to have regained its title of Queen of the Seaside Resorts.

Selected Bibliography

Ayres, Shirley, and Troy Bianchi. *Bradley Beach*. Mount Pleasant, SC: Arcadia, 2004.

Barrett, Richmond. *Good Old Summer Days, Newport, Narragansett Pier, Saratoga, Long Branch, Bar Harbor*. Boston: Houghton Mifflin, 1952.

Beitel, Herb, and Vance Enck. *Cape May County, A Pictorial History*. Virginia Beach, VA: The Donning Company Publishers, 1998.

Boulton, Agnes. *Part of a Long Story*. New York: Doubleday, 1958.

Buchholz, Margaret Thomas, ed. *Shore Chronicles, Diaries and Travelers' Tales from the Jersey Shore, 1764–1955*. Harvey Cedars, NJ: Down The Shore Publishing, 1999.

Burton, Hal. *The Morro Castle*. New York: Viking Press, 1973.

Cappuzzo, Michael. *Close To Shore: A True Story of Terror in an Age of Innocence*. New York: Broadway Books, 2001.

Coad, Oral S. *New Jersey in Travelers' Accounts 1524–1971: A Descriptive Bibliography*. Metuchen, NJ: The Scarecrow Press, Inc., 1972.

Cunningham, John T. *The New Jersey Shore*. New Brunswick, NJ: Rutgers University Press, 1958.

———. *The New Jersey Sampler: Historic Tales of Old New Jersey*. Upper Montclair, NJ: New Jersey Almanac Inc., 1964.

Davis, E. *Atlantic City Diary: A Century of Memories*. Atlantic City, NJ: Atlantic Sunrise Publishing Company, 1985.

Dorsey, Leslie, and Janice Devine. *Fare Thee Well*. New York: Crown Publishers, 1964.

Dorwart, Jeffrey. *Cape May County, N.J.: The Making of an American Resort Community*. New Brunswick, NJ: Rutgers University Press, 1992.

Ellis, Franklin. *History of Monmouth County, New Jersey*. Philadelphia: R. T. Peck and Company, 1885.

Federal Writers' Project of the Works Progress Administration for the State of New Jersey. *Stories of New Jersey*. New York: M. Barrows and Company, 1938.

Fernicola, Richard. *Twelve Days of Terror*. Guilford, CT: The Lyons Press, 2001.

Fraley, Tobin. *The Carousel Animal*. Berkeley, CA: Zephyr Press, 1983.

Francis, David, Diane Francis, and Robert J. Scully Sr. *Wildwood by the Sea: The History of an American Resort*. Fairview Park, OH: Amusement Park Books, 1998.

Funnell, Charles E. *By the Beautiful Sea*. New Brunswick, NJ: Rutgers University Press, 1983.

Futrell, Jim. *Amusement Parks of New Jersey*. Mechanicsburg, PA: Stackpole Books, 2004.

Genovese, Peter. *New Jersey Curiosities*. Guilford, CT: The Globe Pequot Press, 2003.

———. *The Jersey Shore Uncovered: A Revealing Season on the Beach*. New Brunswick, NJ: Rutgers University Press, 2003.

Immerso, Michael. *Coney Island, The People's Playground*. New Brunswick, NJ: Rutgers University Press, 2002.

Johnson, Nelson. *Boardwalk Empire: The Birth, High Times, and Corruption of Atlantic City*. Medford, NJ: Plexus Publishing, Inc., 2002.

Kent, Bill, Robert E. Ruffolo Jr., and Lauralee Dobbins. *Atlantic City, America's Playground*. Carlsbad, CA: Heritage Media Corp., 1998.

Kobbe, Gustav. *The New Jersey Coast and Pines*. New York: Gustav Kobbe Company, 1889.

Lee, Harold. *Ocean City Memories*. Ocean City, NJ: Centennial Commission, 1979.

Levi, Vicki Gold, and Lee Eisenberg. *Atlantic City: 125 Years of Ocean Madness*. New York: Clarkson N. Potter, 1970.

Lloyd, John Bailey. *Eighteen Miles of History of Long Beach Island*. Harvey Cedars, NJ: Down The Shore Publishing, 1986.

McMahon, William. *So Young . . . So Gay! Story of the Boardwalk 1870–1970*. Atlantic City, NJ: Atlantic City Press, 1970.

Miller, Fred. *Ocean City, America's Greatest Family Resort*. Mount Pleasant, SC: Arcadia, 2003.

Moss, George H. Jr. *Steamboat to the Shore*. Locust, NJ: Jersey Close Press, 1966.

Moss, George H. Jr., Karen L. Schnitzspahn, and John T. Cunningham. *Victorian Summers at the Grand Hotels of Long Branch, New Jersey*. Sea Bright, NJ: Ploughshare Press, 2000.

Nowever Then, official Web site of Peter Lucia. *Asbury Park*. www.noweverthen.com /apindex/html.

Roberts, Russell, and Rich Youmans. *Down the Jersey Shore.* New Brunswick, NJ: Rutgers University Press, 1993.

Salvini, Emil R. *The Summer City by the Sea: Cape May, New Jersey— An Illustrated History.* New Brunswick, NJ: Rutgers University Press, 1998.

Santelli, Robert. *The Jersey Shore: A Travel and Pleasure Guide.* Charlotte, NC: The East Woods Press, 1986.

Savadove, Larry, and Margaret Thomas Buchholz. *Great Storms of the Jersey Shore.* Harvey Cedars, NJ: Down The Shore Publishing, 1993.

Scovell, Jane. *Oona, Living in the Shadows. A Biography of Oona O'Neill Chaplin.* New York: Warner Books, 1998.

Stafford, Mike. *I'd Do It All Again . . . But Slower. The Philly/Sea Isle Connection.* (Copy in the Sea Isle City Museum.)

Stansfield, Charles, A. Jr. *Vacationing on the Jersey Shore.* Mechanicsburg, PA: Stackpole Books, 2004.

Sterngass, Jon. *First Resorts, Pursuing Pleasure at Saratoga Springs, Newport & Coney Island.* Baltimore and London: The John Hopkins University Press, 2001.

Waltzer, Jim, and Tom Wilk. *Tales of South Jersey, Profiles and Personalities.* New Brunswick, NJ: Rutgers University Press, 2001.

Wilson, Harold F. *The Story of the Jersey Shore.* Princeton, NJ: D. Van Nostrand Company, Inc., 1964.

———. *The Jersey Shore: A Social and Economic History of the Counties of Atlantic, Cape May, Monmouth and Ocean.* New York and Chicago: Lewis Historical Publishing Company, 1953.

Woolman, H. C., and T. T. Price. *Historical and Biographical Atlas of the New Jersey Coast.* Philadelphia: Woolman and Rose, 1878.

Wortman, Byron C., *The First Fifty: A Biographical History of Seaside Heights.* Edited by George Zuckerman. Seaside Heights, NJ: 50th Anniversary Committee, 1963.

Wrege, Charles D. *Spring Lake, An Early History.* Spring Lake, NJ: Bicentennial History Committee, 1976.

Writers' Program of the Works Progress Administration for the State of New Jersey. *Entertaining a Nation, The Career of Long Branch.* American Guide Series, 1940.

Index

Collection and Photograph Credits

The Author

Emil R. Salvini is a member of the Cape May City Historic Preservation Commission, past president of the North Jersey Highlands Historical Society, and a life member of the Cape May County Historical Society. Author of several books on New Jersey history, this versatile historian is both a careful scholar and an excellent storyteller. He lives with his wife in Wayne, New Jersey, and together they stroll the boardwalks as often as possible.